MOD
CLEAN LIVING UNDER DIFFICULT CIRCUMSTANCES
A VERY BRITISH PHENOMENON

TERRY RAWLINGS
INTRODUCTION BY RICHARD BARNES
THIS BOOK IS DEDICATED TO THE MEMORY OF DAVID WEDGBURY

ISBN: 0.7119.6813.6 ORDER NO: OP 48053

Copyright © 2000 Omnibus Press
(A Division of Book Sales Limited)

Cover & Book designed by Paul McEvoy & Julien Potter at BOLD Graphic Design, London with Terry Rawlings

Picture research by Terry Rawlings

EXCLUSIVE DISTRIBUTORS
Book Sales Limited, 8/9 Frith Street, London W1V 5TZ, UK.

Music Sales Corporation, 257 Park Avenue South, New York, NY 10010, USA.

Music Sales PTY, 4th floor, Usgar House, 30-32 Carrington St, Sydney, NSW 2000, Australia

TO THE MUSIC TRADE ONLY:
Music Sales Limited, 8/9 Frith Street, London W1V 5TZ, UK.

Photo credits:
Every effort has been made to trace the copyright holders of the photographs in this book but one or two were unreachable. We would be grateful if the photographers concerned would contact us.

Printed in Singapore

A catalogue record for this book is available from the British Library. Visit Omnibus Press on the web at www.omnibuspress.com

OMNIBUS PRESS

THE CHASERS: POP ART NE'ER DO WELLS.

INTRODUCTION
Dancing in the street...

Two-tone Tonic, 5" side vents, three-button cuffs, desert boots, French crew, Fred Perry, Hush Puppies, Ski pants, Drynamil, the bang, Charlie & Inez Foxx, Mockingbird. 'Maintain your cool!'

Of all teenage movements, the Mod cult is the only one that years later can be looked back on without any embarrassment. Perhaps youth revolutions should come with a health warning: 'The participant should show some vigilance as he/she might be making a complete prat of him/herself and live to regret it in later life'. Fortunately Mods had no humiliating beads, bondage trousers, flares, phlegm or loon pants to damage their credibility.

Mods are also the only group readily embraced by different generations. Their values have transcended their early Sixties origins and are rediscovered, redeveloped and renewed in 'Mod revivals' with successive tribes of 'New Mods' becoming adept at adopting and adapting from the originals.

Mods are difficult to define. Pete Meaden who introduced me to this then mysterious semi-secret world while transforming the High Numbers into the first ever Mod band, is often quoted as summarising the Mod scene as *"Clean living under difficult circumstances."* Not the slogan of some far right fundamentalist hygiene loonies, but perhaps a clever caption that epitomises the 'attitude' of the early Mods. My own book cover blurb attempt went *"In the early sixties a lifestyle evolved for young people that was mysterious, exciting and fast-moving. It was directed from within and needed no justification from without. Kids were clothes-obsessed, cool, dedicated to R&B and their own dances. They called themselves 'Mods'."*

The words that continually crop up when trying to pinpoint Mods include cool, neat, sharp, hip and smart. The original Sixties Mods evolved from kids growing up in that uncertain, semi-affluent, pivotal period of postwar late Fifties Britain. They were reacting against its repressed, class-obsessed, old maids, warm beer, cold-water, semi-shell-shocked naffness. These were the mind-numbingly empty b&w pre-Beatles dark ages where 'Teenagers', a species that hadn't existed until the Fifties, were simply not catered for. Popular songs still dwelt on over-sentimental 'billing and cooing' and bloated romance hadn't yet been replaced by blatant sex. However it was all about to change.

A handful of discerning British school kids, bored by the faulty pap that was Fifties pop and uninspired by the Skiffle and Trad crazes, aligned with the more sophisticated smoother modern jazz sounds of artists like the Modern Jazz Quartet or Dave Brubeck. They identified with anything then considered new, exciting, controversial and modern – Italian espresso coffee bars, spaghetti bolognaise, moulded plastic, the Comet, the hovercraft and the Mini. Their aspirational fantasy dream pad, somewhere between The Jetsons and early James Bond, would be uncluttered, all-white, minimalist and completely automated with sleek push button sliding panels and doors. These inquisitive radicals embraced all things sexy and streamlined – from the G-plan to the E-type. They became known as Modernists.

Others discarded the dull unflattering British clothes on offer and either made their own or altered the standard issue dross to suit their personal taste. Boys refused the normal severe crude 'short back and sides' male haircut stipulating instead a 'Perry Como' or French crew. They snubbed the clumsy, clunky olive green British BSA Bantam for the sexy cleanlined, streamlined, chromed Italian Vespa or Lambretta.

Mods, unlike their elder brother Teds before them, belonged to the postwar Welfare State generation and were the first to escape having their free spirits broken by Her Majesty's mindless sadists in the press-ganged National Services. Although dismissive of their parents they didn't necessarily want to rebel or change the political status quo. Theirs was a revolt into style, turning their backs on a culture they found dull, timid, old-fashioned and uninspiring. Rather than try to change society they just stuck two well-manicured fingers up at it while strongly urging it to just f-f-fade away (or words to that effect).

While not particularly altruistic, this was long before the sea change of the self-centred, cuntish, coke-cold Eighties and the early Mods, though strictly hedonistic, had a sense of tribal loyalty. They enjoyed that serious Sixties optimism, and, contrary to myth, were friendly, supportive and, the occasional seaside riot apart, surprisingly gentle.

Had these individuals been solely clothes-obsessed they might have become just another small mutual admiration society of trainspotting importance, but somehow, after years of gestation, all the disparate elements arrived at the same place at the same time. Modernists, Individualists, Stylists and Scooter Boys all merged, becoming less purist and more working class. As taste met testosterone they emerged supremely self-confident and streetwise.

It was a very male-led movement, with the girls looking deliberately less feminine as the boys looked deliberately more so. They'd adopted blues, R&B and bluebeat, moved up into clubs and developed their own dances, their own walk and their own attitude. At a time when drugs were yet to become sordid, they cultivated a wider distinctive all-embracing clubland lifestyle with an almost accidental hierarchical structure of Faces and Top Mods calling the changes...

The Modernists had become the Mods.

Rather than try to change society they just stuck two well-manicured fingers up at it while strongly urging it to just f-f-fade away

THE WHO

THE BIRDS

THE BIRDS

THE 'WHO'
LONDON 1965
at THE EALING CLUB from
(OPP. EAL. B'DWAY STN. NEXT TO ABC)
THURS. 4th MARCH

THE
BIRDS
Londons greatest
R. & B. Group

MONDAYS 1, 8, 15, 22, 28 MARCH

7-11. p.m.   .   .   .   .

OPEN SATURDAYS

THE WHO

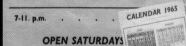
THE BIRDS

THE WHO

modest minor cult
a major minor cult

For a short, intense period during the first half of the Sixties, the Mods, surprisingly, got everything just about right – the music, clothes, hairstyles, dances and the attitude. Fashion obsessed yet not fey. Despite, or because of, no obvious leaders, no media attention, no Sloaney style gurus or pretentious coffee table books like this, these wide-eyed, enthusiastic absolute beginners somehow evolved into the most accomplished, polished, confident, cult sophisticates.

Eventually, the inward looking elusive Mods got their own national showcase. Every Friday evening *Ready Steady Go!* declared, *"...the weekend starts here!"* RSG! was packed with Tamla, R&B and blues artists like Martha and the Vandellas, James Brown, Otis, Supremes, Mary Wells, The Who, The Small Faces etc. It allowed the whole country to see the very latest West End Mod look, hairstyle and new dance. The Mods went public and this once modest minor cult soon evolved into a major minor cult.

Once discovered by the media the term was applied to anything new or quirky, as diverse as fashion designer Mary Quant or *The Avengers* TV series. The term 'Mod' came to represent much more than the 'in' movement of the Sixties. It stood for a particular style and taste. It had come a long way from its early days inspired by the coolness of modern jazz and the chic of Continental fashion. It had produced its own graphic images – Pop Art targets and chevrons – and for many it came to represent more than clothes and music. Its values were applied, among other things, to architecture, design, furniture, graphics, novels etc. and the term is still used today. I'm writing this in the 21st century using an iMac computer, a smooth, neat, speedy, smart, no-nonsense, streamlined, cleanlined machine (and designed by an Englishman). So from The Jetsons to the iMac, forty to fifty years on, the original Mod vision thrives, still with its obsession on all things new, modern and Mod.

Richard Barnes (AUTHOR OF MODS! FIRST PUBLISHED 1979)

ABSOLUTE BEGINNINGS
Flamingo a go-go...

Mods had been seen in and around Soho since 1959 but never in very large numbers. The first reported sightings of fully formed Mods were at the all-night jazz session held at a club called The Flamingo.

Graham Hughes, Paul Stagg and Dicky Dodson were a trio of London's first Mods who were studying at St. Martin's School of Art. Between them they were responsible for adapting and improvising some of the movement's earliest and most enduring styles.

Graham Hughes: *"We were called Modernists to begin with, a term first used by the* Melody Maker *to describe the people that went to the modern jazz clubs like The Flamingo, and listened to artists like Tubby Hayes.*

"We looked different because modern jazz, we felt, was always a bit more stylish and we responded to that. We would go to the allnighter dressed in these box jackets that Cecil Gees imported. They were an Ivy League style, which we wore with a shirt called an American Arrow, which had a button–down collar, which you'd get from a shop called Austins. They actually stocked them specifically for Modernists and this was in 1959.

"It was to look different from the others in the jazz crowd, which was all very studenty, scruffy. We simply didn't want to wear long woolly jumpers and jeans covered in paint. All that happened was that the term Modernist eventually got shortened to Mod".

The Flamingo had begun its club life in the early Fifties as a once-a-week jazz night at another club, The Americana, one of the oldest established music clubs in the West End.

Naturally enough it was to be found in a basement, this time beneath The Mapleton Restaurant in Whitcomb Street, just off Leicester Square. It eventually moved in 1958 to its own full-time premises on Wardour Street, and became one of the most famous venues synonymous with the rise of the early Mod movement.

Once again it was situated in a basement, only this time it was below another club, the celebrity-favoured Whisky A Go Go, a fully licensed society hang-out that attracted London's hippest and highest-profile clientele. All of which contrasted nicely with its unlicensed cellar counterpart whose patrons arrived on scooters and spent the entire night in a dark airless vault listening to modern jazz.

Richard Barnes: *"The Mods never went upstairs because The Whisky was like a proper night club which had a bar, and they were mostly too young anyway, plus it was a pop club like an early Tramp, or the Café de Paris. The Beatles would go there later and people like that. The Mods would go downstairs, which was called The Allnighter. They would meet up there because a lot of Americans would get down there from the air bases and some of them would get up and sing with the bands."*

The Flamingo's strong links with the GIs stretched back to its association with the Americana, which had actually been an American Be Bop club and attracted a large West Indian patronage from all over London, but mainly from the US soldiers stationed in Britain.

When the club moved to Wardour Street, a large proportion of the Americana's customers moved too, especially as The Flamingo had tailored its musical policy to particularly suit them, mixing up its staple modern jazz diet with the healthy addition of early blues and soul of a style championed by Ray Charles and Lee Dorsey. In short, it offered a music menu that catered for both the black market and the Modernists. However, the Mods had an altogether different reason for attending the allnighter — clothes.

Graham Hughes: *"We used to watch Troy Donahue on* Peyton Place *and he had a jacket, a Harrington jacket, a yellow one and Gerry Mulligan and James Dean, who you'd associate with rockers. They had red ones, well Dean did anyway. Harrington jackets were named after*

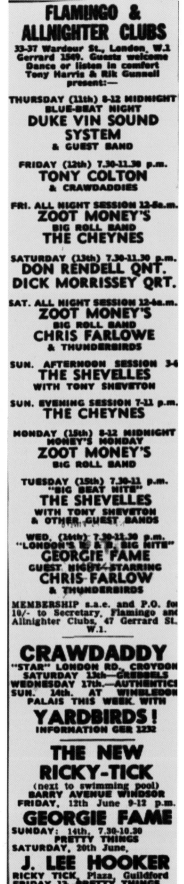

Donahue's character 'Rodney Harrington'. That was the jacket we all wanted. That was the look, white T-shirt, jacket and Levi's. And we got to see that some guys had that look and we couldn't understand where they got the clothes from until someone told us about the allnighters at The Flamingo.

"The GIs would come up to town from the bases, the air bases they were stationed at and before coming into town they would raid their PX store and sell Levi's for a fiver and they had these jackets. You couldn't get this stuff anywhere else. You could get Wranglers and Lee Cooper but you couldn't buy Levi's and certainly not with buttons. They had them with buttons."

The popularity of clubs like the Flamingo was growing but the real Mod explosion was still very much in its smouldering infancy. Soho remained predominantly a very jazz-influenced society and its nightlife reflected that. The majority of the clubs were still dominated by the area's art school students and they in turn set the styles. Dicky Dodson: "What's important to remember is the enormous impact art school had on the shaping of Mod and Soho itself. We were a lot younger than the jazz types who we thought of as scruffy. We liked jazz but American jazz and we wanted a different look. Italian American to begin with and not Paris, France.

"It was impossible to get the clothes — not only for us but for the jazzers as well. They only wore that beatnik style because there wasn't anything alternative. So I suppose they were cool in that respect, to fashion a fashion out of what they could get and it worked but we tried harder and wanted to look smarter.

"We called them Boh's. Big black jumpers down to the knees, which was to cover up trousers which were a mess. They would go down the East End and buy old men's striped business trousers and taper them in so the legs would look OK but the waist and tops were a complete mess. There were cross overs, though. Like the grandad shirts and Chelsea boots, not Beatle boots or winkle pickers, they started differently. Chelsea boots were like Spanish dancing boots.

The real Mod expl... much in its smoul...

was still very
y infancy.

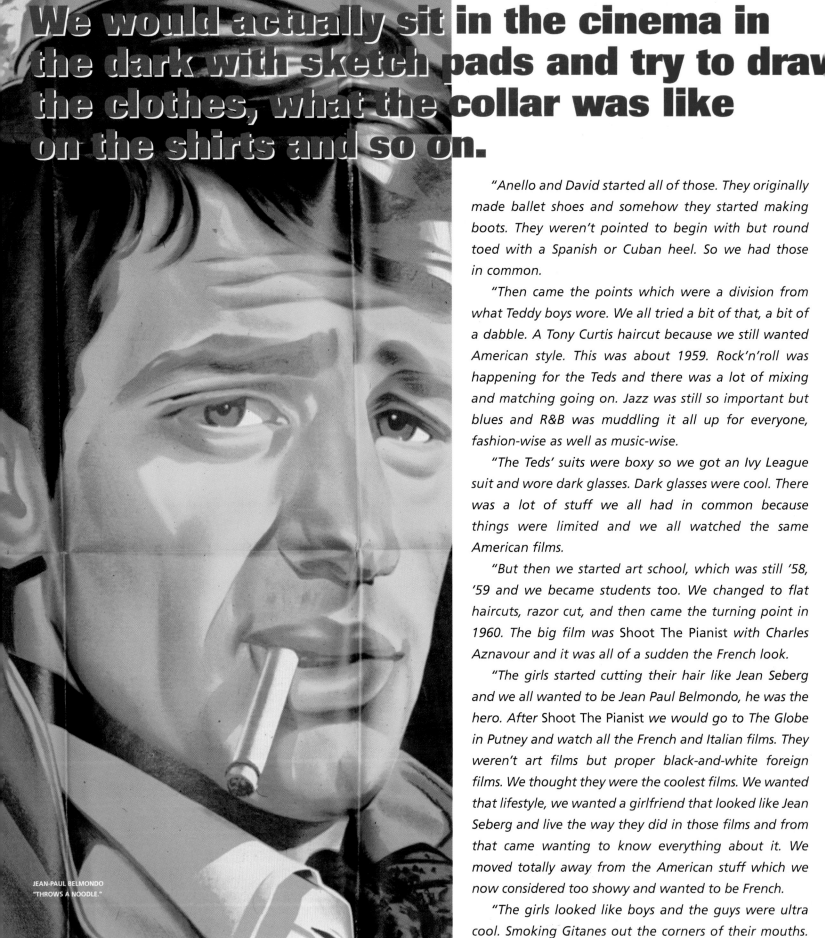

We would actually sit in the cinema in the dark with sketch pads and try to draw the clothes, what the collar was like on the shirts and so on.

JEAN-PAUL BELMONDO
"THROWS A NOODLE."

"Anello and David started all of those. They originally made ballet shoes and somehow they started making boots. They weren't pointed to begin with but round toed with a Spanish or Cuban heel. So we had those in common.

"Then came the points which were a division from what Teddy boys wore. We all tried a bit of that, a bit of a dabble. A Tony Curtis haircut because we still wanted American style. This was about 1959. Rock'n'roll was happening for the Teds and there was a lot of mixing and matching going on. Jazz was still so important but blues and R&B was muddling it all up for everyone, fashion-wise as well as music-wise.

"The Teds' suits were boxy so we got an Ivy League suit and wore dark glasses. Dark glasses were cool. There was a lot of stuff we all had in common because things were limited and we all watched the same American films.

"But then we started art school, which was still '58, '59 and we became students too. We changed to flat haircuts, razor cut, and then came the turning point in 1960. The big film was Shoot The Pianist with Charles Aznavour and it was all of a sudden the French look.

"The girls started cutting their hair like Jean Seberg and we all wanted to be Jean Paul Belmondo, he was the hero. After Shoot The Pianist we would go to The Globe in Putney and watch all the French and Italian films. They weren't art films but proper black-and-white foreign films. We thought they were the coolest films. We wanted that lifestyle, we wanted a girlfriend that looked like Jean Seberg and live the way they did in those films and from that came wanting to know everything about it. We moved totally away from the American stuff which we now considered too showy and wanted to be French.

"The girls looked like boys and the guys were ultra cool. Smoking Gitanes out the corners of their mouths.

GOOD ROCKIN' TONIGHT!

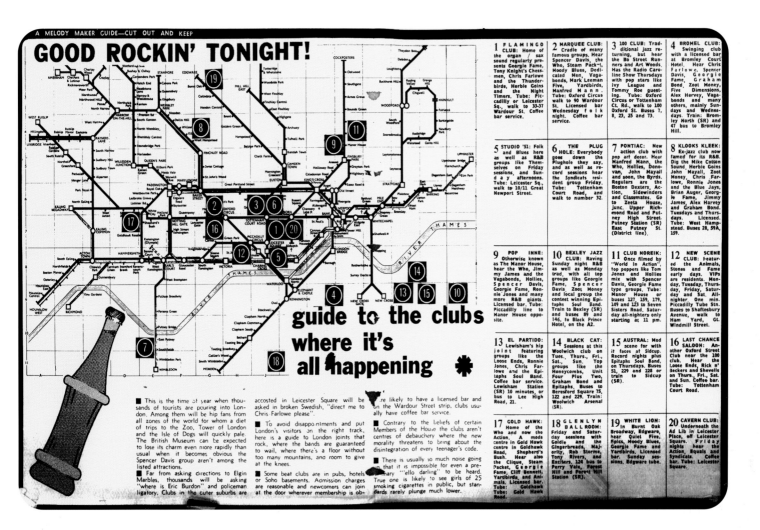

guide to the clubs where it's all happening *

1 FLAMINGO CLUB: Home of the organ sax sound regularly presents Georgie Fame, Tony Knight's Chessmen, Chris Farlowe and the Thunderbirds, Herbie Goins and the Night Timers. Tube: Piccadilly or Leicester Sq., walk to 33-37 Wardour St. Coffee bar service.

2 MARQUEE CLUB: Cradle of many famous groups. Hear Spencer Davis, the Who, Steam Packet, Moody Blues, Dedicated Men, Vagabonds, Mark Leeman Five, Yardbirds, Manfred Mann. Tube: Oxford Circus walk to 90 Wardour St. Licensed bar Wednesday folk night. Coffee bar service.

3 100 CLUB: Traditional jazz returning, but hear the Bo Street Runners and Art Woods. Has the Radio Caroline Show Thursdays with pop stars like Ivy League and Tommy Roe guesting. Tube: Oxford Circus or Tottenham Ct. Rd., walk to 100 Oxford St. Buses 7, 8, 25, 25 and 73.

4 BROMEL CLUB: Swinging club with a licensed bar at Bromley Court Hotel. Hear Chris Farlowe, Spencer Davis, Georgie Fame, Graham Bond, Zoot Money, Five Dimensions, Alex Harvey, Vagabonds and many others, mainly Sundays and Wednesdays. Train: Bromley North (SR) and 47 bus to Bromley Hill.

5 STUDIO '51: Folk and Blues here as well as R&B groups like Themselves on Friday sessions, and Sunday afternoons. Tube: Leicester Sq., walk to 10/11 Great Newport Street.

6 THE PLUG HOLE: Everybody goes down the Plughole they say, and as well as record sessions hear the Syndicats resident group Friday. Tube: Tottenham Court Road, and walk to number 32.

7 PONTIAC: New action club with pop art decor. Hear Manfred Mann, the Who, Hollies, Donovan, John Mayall and soon, the Byrds. Regulars are the Boston Dexters, Action, Sidewinders and Classmates. Go to Zeeta House, junc. Upper Richmond Road and Putney High Street. Putney Station (SR) East Putney St. (District line).

8 KLOOKS KLEEK: Ex-jazz club now famed for its R&B. Dig the Mike Cotton Sound, Herbie Goins John Mayall, Zoot Money, Chris Farlowe, Ronnie Jones and the Blue Jays, Brian Auger, Georgie Fame, Jimmy James, Alex Harvey and Graham Bond. Tuesdays and Thursdays. Licensed. Tube: West Hampstead. Buses 28, 59A, 159.

9 POP INNE: Otherwise known as The Manor House, hear the Who, Jimmy James and the Vagabonds, Hollies, Spencer Davis, Georgie Fame, Ronnie Jones and many more R&B giants. Licensed bar. Tube: Piccadilly line to Manor House opposite.

10 BEXLEY JAZZ CLUB: Raving Sunday night R&B as well as Monday trad, with all top groups like Georgie Fame, Spencer Davis Zoot Money and local group the contest winning Epitaphs Soul Band. Train to Bexley (SR) and buses 89 and 146, to Black Prince Hotel, on the A2.

11 CLUB NOREIK: Once filmed by "World In Action" top poppers like Tom Jones and Hollies mix with Spencer Davis, Georgie Fame type groups. Tube: Manor House or buses 127, 159, 179, 149 and 123 to Seven Sisters Road. Saturday all-nighters only starting at 11 pm.

12 NEW SCENE CLUB: Featured the Animals, Stones and Fame early days. VIPs are residents. Monday, Tuesday, Thursday, Friday, Saturday and Sat. All-nighter. One min. Piccadilly Tube Stn. Buses to Shaftesbury Avenue, walk to Ham Yard, Gt. Windmill Street.

13 EL PARTIDO: Lewisham's hip joint featuring groups like the Loose Ends, Ronnie Jones, Chris Farlowe and the Epitaphs Soul Band. Coffee bar service. Lewisham Station (SR) 10 minutes, or bus to Lee High Road, 21.

14 BLACK CAT: Sessions at this Woolwich club on Tues., Thurs., Fri., Sat., Sun. Top groups like the Honeycombs, Unit Four Plus Two, Graham Bond and Epitaphs, Buses to Beresford Square 75, 122 and 229. Train: Woolwich Arsenal (SR).

15 AUSTRAL: Mod scene for with it faces at Sidcup. Record nights plus Epitaphs Soul Band, on Thursdays. Buses 51, 229 and 228 or train to Sidcup (SR).

16 LAST CHANCE SALOON: Another Oxford Street club near the 100 club. Hear the Loose Ends, Rick n' Beckers and Shevells on Thurs., Fri., Sat. and Sun. Coffee bar. Tube: Tottenham Court Road.

17 GOLD HAWK: Home of the Who and now the Action. A mods centre in the Gold Hawk centre in Goldhawk Road, Shepherd's Bush. Hear also the Clique, Steam Packet, Georgie Fame, Cliff Bennett, Yardbirds and Animals. Licensed bar. Tube: Goldhawk Tube: Gold Hawk Road.

18 GLENLYN BALL ROOM: Friday and Saturday sessions with Goldie and the Gingerbreads, Majority, Rob Storme, Tony Rivers, and Exciters, 124 bus to Perry Vale, Forest Hill and Forest Hill Station (SR).

19 WHITE LION: In Burnt Oak Broadway, Edgware, hear Quiet Five, Epics, Moody Blues, Georgie Fame and Yardbirds. Licensed bar. Sunday sessions, Edgware tube.

20 CAVERN CLUB: Underneath the Ad Lib in Leicester Place, off Leicester Square. Friday nights hear the Action, Equals and Syndicats. Coffee bar. Tube: Leicester Square.

■ This is the time of year when thousands of tourists are pouring into London. Among them will be hip fans from all zones of the world for whom a diet of trips to the Zoo, Tower of London and the Isle of Dogs will quickly pale. The British Museum can be expected to lose its charm even more rapidly than usual when it becomes obvious the Spencer Davis group aren't among the listed attractions.

■ Far from asking directions to Elgin Marbles, thousands will be asking "where is Eric Burdon" and policeman ligatory, Clubs in the cuter suburbs are accosted in Leicester Square will be asked in broken Swedish, "direct me to Chris Farlowe please".

■ To avoid disappointments and put London's visitors on the right track, here is a guide to London joints that rock, where the bands are guaranteed to wail, where there's a floor without too many mountains, and room to give at the knees.

■ Some beat clubs are in pubs, hotels or Soho basements. Admission charges are reasonable and newcomers can join at the door wherever membership is ob-

...re likely to have a licensed bar and on the Wardour Street strip, clubs usually have coffee bar service.

■ Contrary to the beliefs of certain Members of the House the clubs aren't centres of debauchery where the new morality threatens to bring about the disintegration of every teenager's code.

■ There is usually so much noise going on that it is impossible for even a pre-nary "'ello darling" to be heard. True one is likely to see girls of 25 smoking cigarettes in public, but standards rarely plunge much lower.

ALEXIS & CYRIL.

Playing t
blocks, y

Alain Delon had a scooter, he was in Paris and he had a girl on the back. Fuck me, what more could you want? We would notice every little detail, details of our heroes. It got totally obsessive, our behaviour was obsessive and completely took us over. It got so bad that the film didn't matter. What mattered was seeing what Belmondo or Delon was wearing and knowing we couldn't get it so we would have to improvise.

"We would actually sit in the cinema in the dark with sketch pads and try to draw the clothes, what the collar was like on the shirts, how far the lapel was away from the shoulder and so on. Luckily we were art students so the drawings weren't too bad in the daylight!

"You would pull up outside a club on your scooter and never say a word, you never pulled anybody. Never bothered with small talk, that was so uncool. You just stood by the door and found something to lean against. We saw one film with Belmondo where he was doing something with his lip so we all did it. We called it 'throwing a noodle'. The girls would go to see the same films and eventually we'd bump into girls who knew about the same stuff we did and this was in the East End. The East End girls were so cool."

Meanwhile R&B in 1962 was alive and well and appearing nightly to a packed Ealing club crowd, courtesy of Blues Incorporated and friends. By May of that year the Tiny Little Teashop basement, had already played host to the emerging talents of Mick Jagger, Keith Richard, Eric Clapton and Paul Jones. This was all within two months of opening its doors and at a time when the band's own revolving roster had proudly and regularly presented the likes of bass player Jack Bruce, drummer Charlie Watts, a saxophone player Dick Heckstall Smith and on vocals Jagger himself. However, one of the most impressionable and ambitious young men to have followed Blues Incorporated — and Korner's career in particular (from his days with Chris Barber's Band) — was a kid from Cheltenham called Brian Jones. Jones was in London in order to form his own band whose members he would recruit, bar one, from either Blues Incorporated itself or from the Ealing Club audience. He would call them The Rolling Stones.

The Ealing club was a watershed. Even though the band formed by Korner and Davies stayed in residence for only a little under a year, they proved that given the right circumstances and a determined group, R&B could be enormously popular. It was almost as if that little club had acted as an incubator, nurturing and strengthening R&B until its potential could be fully unleashed, and made strong enough to leave the suburbs and return to its roots in Soho. Which was exactly what it did. When Blues Incorporated returned to the West End that same year it played to a full house crowd that included the entire Ealing contingent at The Marquee Club in Oxford Street.

Thus The Marquee became the crucible in which Mod and Soho's music scene developed. The club eventually took on a legendary status due in part to its original and unique talent-spotting policy. This was implemented by encouraging new and unsigned bands to play the club as an unpaid interval act, in pretty much the same way Blues Incorporated had done. These bands could therefore play once a week for an entire month, in an effort to build up a following — assuming they were any good, of course.

bs was like doing it with building
ilt up slowly and certain rules applied.

If the response was positive enough the band could then play a support spot and then finally headline. This policy was later updated and simplified and the interval spot was replaced by an actual support spot. These bands could play an entire set, get their name on the bill and even get paid. Eventually the Marquee support slot becoming one of the most important live stepping stones for any up-and-coming band to play in London.

Billy Hasset of The Chords: *"Playing The Marquee was seen as the big time, it was the West End club to play and you knew you could not headline there unless you had played support. It became very important, almost a graduation thing, a hurdle to overcome on the route to bigger things. Quite amazing. Playing the clubs was like doing it with building blocks, you built up slowly and certain rules applied. It was serious stuff."*

The Who, Jeff Beck, The Move, Clayton Squares, David Bowie and The Spencer Davis Group all played support slots at the club during the Sixties and all acknowledge the club as a pivotal moment in their career. Well, maybe not The Clayton Squares...

"The mods are responsible as principal consumers for the progress of pop music and the tabernacle and heart of London's blood music is The Marquee Club at 90 Wardour Street, W1," wrote Len Deighton in his London Dossier. *"The entrance is murky and the air inside is hot, damp and salty. If you really like pop music and can survive in unconditioned air you should investigate.*

"The audience sits (the club had rows of sofas) *in rows, attentive, and the groups come from all over England and if they make it at The Marquee, that's the big break. The management here has recording studios and can help and promote a favoured group.*

"The faces in the audience are very beautiful 15 year olds, untouched by anything more than cool, no one screams here, they don't even smile, you can see the fantasies in their eyes but there isn't time to speak between numbers. No one dances much. The groups have an act, they are not dance bands."

The Marquee remained on Oxford Street until 1964 when it moved a few hundred yards to a new site on Wardour Street. The new plot turned out to be crown land and the club's opening was delayed for several weeks while a special dispensation order was obtained to allow live music and a bar.

The club finally reopened on March 13, 1964, and featured debut night entertainment from The Yardbirds, Sonny Boy Williamson (backed by The Yardbirds) and Long John Baldry, ably backed up by his Hoochie Coochie Men. More about these later, for now it's back to the Mods.

The faces in the audience are very beautiful 15 year old untouched by anythi more than cool.

marquee club

GERRARD 8923 | 90, WARDOUR STREET, LONDON W.1.

MAR. 1966 Programme

Tue. 1st	**MANFRED MANN** **The D. J. Blues Band** (Members: 6/– Non-members: 8/6) *Members' tickets in advance from February 22nd
Wed. 2nd	**CHRIS BARBER'S JAZZ BAND** with Kenneth Washington **RAM HOLDER BROS.** (Members: 5/– Non-members: 7/6)
Thur. 3rd	Jimmy James and the **VAGABONDS** **THE SUMMER SET**
Fri. 4th	**GARY FARR and the T-BONES** **The Objects**
Sat. 5th	Modern Jazz: **RONNIE ROSS QUARTET** **TONY KINSEY QUINTET**
Sun. 6th	**SUNDAY FOLK SPECIAL** Davy Graham, Max and John Le mont and Marilla Waesche (Members: 5/6 Non-members: 6/6)
Mon. 7th	**GRAHAM BOND** Organisation **Felder's Orioles**
Tue. 8th	**SPENCER DAVIS GROUP** **The Explosive JIMMY CLIFF** (Members: 6/– Non-members: 8/6) *Members' tickets in advance from March 8th
Wed. 9th	**3 City 4, Al Stewart Backwater 4**
Thur. 10th	**MARK LEEMAN FIVE** **THE SUMMER SET**
Fri. 11th	From the U.S.A.: **IRMA THOMAS and her Group** **Roscoe Brown Combo**
Sat. 12th	Modern Jazz: **DICK MORRISSEY QUARTET** **RAY WARLEIGH QUARTET**
Sun. 13th	**CLOSED**
Mon. 14th	**THE STEAM PACKET** **Long John Baldry, Rod Stewart, Julie Driscoll, Brian Auger Trinity Target 66**
Tue. 15th	The Return of **THE YARDBIRDS** **The Clayton Squares** (Members: 6/– Non-members: 8/6) *Members' tickets in advance from March 8th
Wed. 16th	**THE SPINNERS** **New Harvesters, Mike Rogers**
Thur. 17th	**MARK LEEMAN FIVE** **The Objects**
Fri. 18th	**DAVID BOWIE and the BUZZ** **THE SUMMER SET**
Sat. 19th	Modern Jazz: **DICK MORRISSEY QUARTET** **TONY KINSEY QUINTET**
Sun. 20th	**JAZZ 625 (B.B.C.-T.V.)** Members only. Tickets available free on personal application one week prior to this date.
Mon. 21st	Jimmy James and the **VAGABONDS** **BOZ and the SIDEWINDERS**
Tue. 22nd	First appearance at the Marquee: **THE SMALL FACES** **The Summer Set** (Members: 6/– Non-members: 8/6) *Members' tickets in advance from March 15th
Wed. 23rd	**RAM HOLDER BROS.** **Jo Ann Kelly, Shades of Blue**
Thur. 24th	**MARK LEEMAN FIVE** **Roscoe Brown Combo**
Fri. 25th	**GARY FARR and the T-BONES** **Alan Walker Group**
Sat. 26th	Modern Jazz: **DICK MORRISSEY QUARTET** **JOHNNY SCOTT QUINTET**
Sun. 27th	**To be announced** **Watch the "M.M." for details**
Mon. 28th	**MIKE COTTON SOUND** with Lucas **The D.J. Blues Band**
Tue. 29th	**THE ACTION** **The Loose Ends** *Members' tickets in advance from March 22nd
Wed. 30th	**THE FRUGAL SOUND** **New Harvesters, The Compromise**
Thur. 31st	**MARK LEEMAN FIVE** **Bo Street Runners**

Every Saturday afternoon, 2.30–5.30 p.m.

"THE SATURDAY SHOW"
**Top of the Pops both Live and on Disc
Introduced by Guest D.Js.,
featuring Star Personalities**

Members: 3/6   Non-members: 4/6

(All Programmes are subject to alteration and the Management
cannot be held responsible for non-appearance of artists.)

ON YER BIKE

Another often overlooked but important influence on early Mod fashions came not from romantic Paris, courtesy of Belmondo and his pals, but from the Fulham Road and an Italian cycling shop called Barry Harmonds. The shop was half owned by the Bertorelli family, the proprietors of several Italian restaurants throughout London, and it sold imported Italian racing bikes and sports wear.

Graham Hughes: *"Everything came from graphics and cycling is very graphic. Cycling was so influential on the first Mods, terrifically so, and it dates back to Junior Art School, at Christopher Wren in Notting Hill Gate. You went there at 13 and that's where we all met. Everyone had bikes to go to school, mostly British bikes like a Holdsworth but if you were cool you rode a Tremelli or any Italian import. So that competition element was already there or 'Topping Up' as it would be known later. The whole cycling style derived from back then.*

"We carried it on to when we were Mods. You followed the Tour de France and all our heroes were Italian cyclists, basically because they were foreign. Our sporting heroes ranked alongside our cinema heroes. Not English footballers or cricketers like most other teenagers were into, we adopted cyclists. Instead of Stanley Matthews, I had Louie Jean Balvet and Fausto Cockpee. It was just to be different and because they looked good. It had style. You'd buy all the Italian newspapers from Solosisis in Charing Cross Road, an Italian newsagents that would have papers and sports papers imported for the Italian community that stretched up from Clerkenwell in to the West End. Enormous, great broadsheets that had pages and pages of cycling and racing. The haircuts came from Pete's, an Italian hairdresser at the back of Rathbone Place. He could do the haircut with the parting, no gel. Razor cut and tapered. You would go there and he had all these pictures of cyclists right round the wall, with these great haircuts.

"Racing tops were only worn when you raced. It was totally uncool to wear a racing top in the street then.

That came much later. But the berets came out of that time.

"Mods wore berets because these papers had pictures of cyclists racing in the winter and training out of racing jerseys. Wonderful, roll collar jumpers with a beret and dark glasses.

"We had to adapt the look to get the best results and because we all had a graphics background, we came at cycling with the graphic in mind. You could get the racing jerseys and in those days they had collars on them. They weren't crew neck like they are now. You couldn't buy that polo shirt look in the UK. The French and Italians had them a long time before us. So if you wore a cycling shirt in a plain colour under a V-neck sweater you could get that polo look and a lot of those tops were knitted so it worked really well.

"You weren't cool if you stuck out, you were cool by the detail. The detail is what stuck out, got you noticed. The way you walked had to have attitude. And then people would look at detail. 'Aaah look at that jacket look at those trousers, shirt, haircut and look at his girlfriend.' You would try and look like a movie star but subtly.

"One shop in particular started the whole idea of fashion being in vogue and it was called Courtney Reeds, that was the first shop that started to sell clothes that were different to everywhere else.

"They had underwear and sold knickers, girls' knickers, that were actually sexy, before anywhere else even thought about displaying them. It was considered gay or camp because this was in 1958. You could get a little catalogue and it was as close to being able to buy a porn book you could get. Everyone I knew got those brochures. It was the only shop, before Carnaby Street or Kings Road. John Michaels came next and eventually Mary Quant, then all the rest.

"John Stevens was another. He opened up his first shop in Fulham. The smallest shop you've ever seen in your life. It was originally an estate agents. Really tiny. It had one shirt in its window. And you could pay on the book. I got to know him really well. My mum asked me what I wanted for Christmas and I said I wanted this shirt and she went down there and gave him half a crown a week, every week for months until Christmas. He then moved to Carnaby Street."

By July '62, Blues Incorporated were a big enough live draw throughout the south of England to attract the attention of BBC Radio, who put out a weekly live jazz show called Jazz Club. The offer was the band's biggest break to date and Korner, naturally, leapt at the chance. There was one slight problem, however. The broadcast clashed with the band's Thursday night residency at The Marquee and as Thursday nights were now the club's most profitable, Harold Pendleton refused them the night off. *"No gig, no residency"*, he announced unobligingly. Korner came up with a solution. Vocalist Jagger was no longer fronting Blues Incorporated as regularly as he had once done; Art Wood now had the job pretty much full-time. Instead, Jagger had thrown in his lot with Brian Jones, in the latter's fledgling R&B venture The Rolling Stones.

Korner reasoned with Pendleton that if the Jagger-fronted Stones filled in for Blues Incorporated, the audience wouldn't be too put out if the rest of the line-up was different. After all, the singer had been a familiar face within the band. Pendleton sceptically agreed to Korner's somewhat shaky proposition and granted them the night off.

On July 11, 1962, *Jazz News* ran an ad in its weekly gig guide announcing that, *"Mick Jagger, R&B vocalist, is taking a Rhythm and Blues group called The Rolling Stones into The Marquee tomorrow night, while Blues Incorporated is doing the Jazz Club radio show"*.

Thus The Rolling Stones prepared for their first ever public appearance. It was tough going. The club's large contingent of die-hard jazz buffs had been quietly respectful of Blues Inc.'s brand of professionalism, if not their actual choice of music, but they were decidedly miffed at paying out good money to watch a scruffy bunch of long-haired fadsters.

The atmosphere became even more charged when mid-way through the Stones' set, a large crowd of Mods, unaware of the change in circumstances, entered the club and became openly contemptuous of the predominantly goatee-bearded audience. They barged their way to the front of the stage and, inspired by the group's driving R&B and Brian and Keith Richards' Muddy Waters riffing, got sufficiently carried away to start a punch-up.

Understandably, Pendleton was put out by the violence. A director of the National Jazz Association, he was keen to promote The Marquee's image as a law-abiding venue. Having made the mistake of booking the Stones without seeing or hearing them play a single note, he rapidly came to the conclusion that he'd made a big mistake. He made it clear to the Stones, and to Korner, that he held them all responsible for tarnishing both his and the club's reputation, and informed them that he would think long and hard before inviting Jagger's lot back again. Nevertheless, the band considered the gig a success. The fighting Mods had only added to the band's raw and untapped energy while unwittingly kick-starting the Stones' dangerous live reputation.

Richard Barnes: *"The Rolling Stones played R&B but mixed it up with Chuck Berry and Bo Diddley material. They built up a big, big Mod following, but eventually they (the Mods) went off them. Their first single was a dodgy cover of Chuck Berry's 'Come On', which wasn't particularly good. I think that turned a lot of them off."*

Mods only really liked the originals and the Stones commercialised coveted Mod favourites, which was considered sacrilege. The Stones were also regarded as a scruffy lot, though they were considered infinitely preferable to The Beatles.

Ken Browne: *"Mods hated The Beatles and they completely ignored Mersey Beat. Mersey Beat was thought of as girl's music, pop, Top Ten stuff. It never really caught on in the London clubs or anywhere in the south of England. We fucking hated The Beatles, we only liked the Stones up to a point. The Beatles were a girls' group, there's no doubt about that. They invented nothing clotheswise. The only thing they did was let somebody take the collar off the jackets, that we thought was brilliant. OK you live and learn and you eventually realise they were great, but at the time you didn't give them a second thought."*

MEMBERSHIP CARD
MUST BE SHOWN FOR ADMISSION
SOUTHALL JIVING CLUB
WHITE HART HOTEL, SOUTHALL
Every Friday & Saturday Evening
NOT TRANSFERABLE
SIGNATURE B.P.Dunn
TO THE MANAGEMENT BELONGS THE RIGHT OF REFUSING ADMISSION

MEMBERSHIP CARD
MUST BE SHOWN FOR ADMISSION
SOUTHALL SUNDAY CLUB
EXPIRING 31st DECEMBER 1965
MEMBERSHIP 1/- PER ANNUM
NOT TRANSFERABLE
SIGNATURE B.P.Dunn
TO THE MANAGEMENT BELONGS THE RIGHT OF REFUSING ADMISSION

MEMBERSHIP CARD
MUST BE SHOWN FOR ADMISSION
SOUTHALL SUNDAY CLUB
EXPIRING 31st DECEMBER 1964
NOT TRANSFERABLE
SIGNATURE B.P.Dunn
TO THE MANAGEMENT BELONGS THE RIGHT OF REFUSING ADMISSION

ZAMBEZI

(opposite Hounslow Bus Station)

8 TILL LATE

MARCH 18th——STEAM PACKET
   ,,   25th——VAGABONDS

APRIL 1st——MARK LEEMAN 5
   ,,   8th——ZOOT MONEY
   ,, 15th——JOHN MAYALL
   ,, 22nd——RAM-JAM-BAND
   ,, 29th——CHRIS FARLOW

MAY 6th——NITETIMERS

EVERY FRIDAY NIGHT

SOUTHALL COMMUNITY CENTRE 1966
CENTRE BEAT CLUB
EVERY SUNDAY 7.30 - 10.30 p.m.

YOUR CARD MUST BE PRODUCED
ON EACH VISIT BEFORE ADMISSION

LOST CARDS MUST BE REPLACED COST 1/-
Right of Admission Strictly Reserved

MEMBERSHIP CARD
'Zambezi' Club 1965
(HOUNSLOW)
Name Beverly Dunn
Address 19, Romney Rd
Hayes
Middx
EXPIRY DATE 31.12.65

100 CLUB
100 OXFORD ST. W.1
7.30 to 11 p.m.
RHYTHM AND BLUES

Thursday, April 16th
GRAHAM BOND'S ORGANISATION
JOHN LEE and the GROUND HOGS
THE CLOUDS

Monday, April 20th
THE MIKE COTTON SOUND
BRIAN KNIGHTS BLUES BY SIX
THE POPULARS

Tuesday, April 21st
THE PRETTY THINGS
THE ART WOOD COMBO
THE IMPACTS

Thursday, April 23rd
GRAHAM BOND'S ORGANISATION
JOHN LEE and the GROUND HOGS
THE CONTINENTALS

Full details of the Club from the Secretary
100 Club, 22 Newman St., W.1 (LAN 0184)

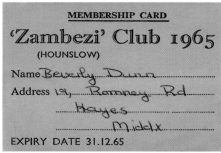

KLOOKS KLEEK
No. 22279
jazz at the
RAILWAY HOTEL
west hampstead
SIGNATURE: S. Carrigall

The DOG-HOUSE Club
HARROW WEALD MEMORIAL HALL
EVERY MONDAY
Membership Card 1965
Member's Signature B.P.Dunn
Address 19 Romney Rd, Hayes, Middx
STRICTLY NOT TRANSFERABLE

Goldhawk Social Beat Club
(*DANCING*)
MEMBERSHIP CARD
MUST BE SHOWN FOR ADMISSION

NOT TRANSFERABLE
EXPIRING 31st DEC. 1965

SIGNATURE B.P.Dunn
(I am over 18 years of age)

In the meantime the Stones, in line with their cover of the Arthur Alexander hit 'You Better Move On', had secured their own regular night at the Ealing Club, before moving to The Station Hotel in Richmond and then to the bigger Richmond Athletic clubhouse, all within a few short months. Such was their meteoric rise in popularity that a return to The Marquee was inevitable. However, it also proved to be short-lived, largely because Keith Richards expressed his dislike of Harold Pendelton by hitting him over the head with his guitar. It was the end of any future Stones-Marquee collaborations and confirmation of the band's bad boy reputation.

Ken Browne: *"The Stones were too big for the Ealing club dates even in '63 and they gave up the gig to go on tour with Bo Diddley. The Yardbirds took over and the Mods loved them. They played authentic R&B and Eric Clapton was a Mod. He was a Levi Mod, not a suit Mod. He wore desert boots and had his hair done with the parting. He had the proper Levi's look. You could tell he took care of them. The care you took with your Levi's was unbelievable. When you washed your Levi's you didn't just put them in a washing machine, you used to get them on the draining board and you would scrub the knee, and scrub the fly so you would get the ring coming through the button. The knees and crutch had to be white. That, believe it or not, was the look.*

"My brother used to go and clean his scooter and I remember our mum saying to me 'Why is he cleaning his bike in his suit?' and I said 'So he doesn't muck up his Levi's, he only has to go to work in his suit.'

"To keep the legs dead straight in Levi's we used to cut out two pieces of wood exactly to size, wash the jeans, wring them out and push the wood up the legs so they would dry dead straight. They were that important because you couldn't go out and simply buy another pair."

The Marquee experience may have been the end of small club-size performances by the Stones, but it wasn't the end of their experiences with Mods, or Mod violence for that matter.

On April 8, 1964, the Stones headlined the Ready Steady Go! Mad Mod Ball at the Empire Pool, Wembley.

Described at the time as the most ambitious outdoor event ever undertaken, it was the brainwave of Elkan Allan, the entertainment chief for Associated Rediffusion and the man responsible for the weekly live TV show. Allan and *Ready Steady Go!*'s editor, Francis Hitching, decided to take the show's winning studio format and recreate it outside.

Top secret talks were held and plans were laid out under the code name 'Operation Mod'. The acts booked to appear were The Searchers, Sounds Incorporated, The Mersey Beats, The Fourmost, Cilla Black, Kathy Kirby, Billy J. Kramer, The Dakotas, Freddie & The Dreamers, Manfred Mann and Kenny Lynch. Topping the bill were The Rolling Stones.

Ready Steady Go!'s regular hosts Keith Fordyce, Michael Aldred and Cathy McGowan would MC the event and a special announcement was made on the March 6 edition of the show, informing everyone that tickets were available at £1 10s, and the money was to go to children's charities. Eight thousand tickets went on sale, six thousand seated and two thousand standing and the audience was requested to attend the event dressed in "bizarre Mod fashions". Every ticket was sold out by March 9 after an unprecedented 25,000 requests were made.

Although a commercial success, the event descended into chaos when rival gangs of Mods and Rockers attacked each other and fought a pitched battle in front of the stage housing The Rolling Stones. Police reinforcements were called in and over 30 arrests were made in the arena. The riot was so bad the band were left stranded on the podium for 30 minutes before order was restored. The Stones' reputation for attracting trouble was up and running.

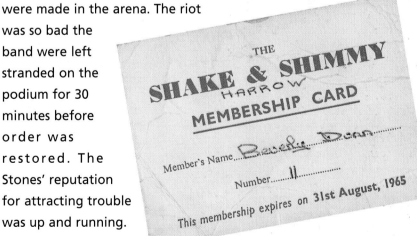

There was a strong chance that so...

SOHO & BOHOS
London's Mod music roots...

The genuine Mod was as fastidious about his music as he was about his clothes, and to trace the roots of Mod music it is necessary to travel way beyond the obvious Sixties, back as far as the Forties and not to a particular person but to a place, Soho in Central London.

Soho has always been something of an oddity. Located at the heart of the sprawling metropolis that is London, it somehow manages to retain the atmosphere of a small, village-like community; and yet at the same time it's totally cosmopolitan. From as far back as the Thirties, when its mass of late night cafés, bars, restaurants and pubs lured notable tenants such as Evelyn Waugh and Dylan Thomas to the area, it has been eternally in vogue with the country's literary and artistic life. Waugh and Thomas mingled with the likes of Julian Maclaren-Ross and Ruthven Todd, both of whom were instrumental in the resurgence of publishing individual poetry in London. They founded the *London Press Magazine* and for a whole surge of poets and writers, Soho became their own private Bohemia, setting a trend that shows no sign of abating even today.

It was during the Second World War that the area received its most stimulating impetus. Into Soho gravitated the American serviceman — hundreds of GIs, sailors and flyboys, all of them desperate for some after hours fun on their infrequent days on leave. They naturally inspired a healthy black market trade in many of Uncle Sam's finest consumables and, thanks to the existence of several air bases left in place by the US on the outskirts of London, such as Ruislip and Eastcote, would continue to do so well after the war.

This marked the beginning of England's gradual process of Americanisation. Its flames fanned by the hunger of a deprived postwar generation of British youth, Americanisation was welcomed unconditionally, particularly amongst Soho's nonconforming art school students of the Fifties.

These youngsters called themselves beats, or, like their US counterparts, beatniks, and they were probably one of the first teenage, for want of a better word, cults to hit Britain. They were bohemian basement dwellers, pipe smokers and subterranean political activists. CND membership was mandatory — which tended to annoy the service-men in Soho — and there was a strong chance that some of their girlfriends might 'go all the way'. Poetry and chess were in and they even had their own language — so get hip daddy 'O'!

The beatniks brought to the area, and helped to popularise, a distinctive musical element: jazz. For the beatniks, give or take the odd bongo basher, were fanatical jazz buffs, inventing the allnighter, Trad jazz clubs and to a large extent the all-night coffee bar.

The coffee bar, as opposed to cafe, was a small, smoke-filled, alcohol-free meeting place that catered almost exclusively to the young jazzers and GIs of Soho, at the heart of which was the gleaming chrome spectacle of the espresso coffee machine.

their girlfriends might 'go all the way'.

The first to boast such a facility was the Moka in Frith Street. It was so successful that it sparked a chain reaction that saw coffee bars open literally overnight, often within yards of each other. Bars with names like Heaven And Hell, The Partisan and Le Macabre (which lived up to its name by fashioning coffee tables out of coffin lids), provided a perfect accompaniment to the slightly older and more expensive jazz 'club' scene.

This centred around venues such as Club II, Cy Laurie's jazz club (the original allnighter, made possible by its no-alcohol policy), and the Humphrey Lyttleton Club which was located in the basement of 100 Oxford Street. There was also Studio 51, renamed The Colyer Club whenever band leader Ken Colyer was in residency, and The Mandrake. All added to Soho's 24-hour pace.

In 1955, as a celebration of the area's vibrancy, a summer festival was organised by the residents' society (The Soho Association) in an effort to spotlight Soho's many positive and healthy aspects — as opposed to the seedy and vice-ridden image painted by the media.

It was a week-long street party featuring the biggest names on the jazz and literary scene. George Melly, Chris Barber, John Dankworth and Ken Colyer played free from the backs of brightly decorated floats designed by students from the local St. Martin's School of Art. Parades snaked around the narrow streets, poetry readings were held in Soho Square and music blared out of every doorway. It would run annually for four years and prove such a popular London attraction that the local council felt duty bound to abolish it in 1960.

By then Soho's musical climate was changing dramatically. Although the tide was slow to turn and reactionaries would oppose it in the way that King Canute opposed the waves, musicians such as Chris Barber and Cyril Davies were leaning more towards jazz's bastard offshoots, blues and skiffle.

Although essentially a trad trombonist, Barber had a keen business sense and welcomed any musical development that might further his band's popularity. As a result he had started including blues and skiffle in his set as far back as 1950, interrupting his big band's programme in order to introduce a segregated quintet within it.

These five musicians, which included guitar players Alexis Korner and Tony 'Lonnie' Donegan, would play a short interval piece that they coined a skiffle set, after an American form of music that dated back to the Thirties. Skiffle was a term used to describe the entertainment provided to raise money at rent parties during the depression, an early stripped-down acoustic version of rhythm & blues that owed its origins to old-style Mississippi bluegrass and country. The instrumentation was at best makeshift, suggesting that its earliest exponents were poor but inventive. Packing crates and half barrels were used as basses, cigar boxes became guitars, and washboards, paper combs and kazoos normally backed up the bottle and jug blowers. Basically, whatever was at hand was utilised and added to the musical melée in what was really the earliest form of jamming. These British skiffle intermissions were so successful that pretty soon skiffle bands were forming around the West End, among them The Ken Colyer Skiffle Group, which for a time also included Korner. The latter recorded over seven tracks for Decca before, like Donegan before him, he went it alone.

ALEXIS KORNER.

There will be precious little trade in second-hand music shops by the en

Donegan, with Barber's backing, was the first skiffle musician to score a Top 20 hit in 1956 with a commercial rendition of Leadbelly's 'Rock Island Line', and this led the way for even more skiffle acts to follow. Most notable were The Vipers, who also hit big with 'Don't You Rock Me Daddy "O"' and at one time or another featured three future Shadows in Hank B. Marvin, Jet Harris and Tony Meehan, all backing the singer Wally Whyton, and guitarist Chas McDevitt with his hit version of 'Freight Train'. Like the coffee bars before them, skiffle clubs were now the hot hang-outs. Clubs like The Good Earth, Richards and The Skiffle Cellar all catered to a thriving scene that in pre-Beatles London divided Soho's music community down the middle.

But the most famous of them all was The 2Is (pronounced 'two eyes'), a ground-floor coffee bar and basement skiffle bar on the south side of Old Compton Street close to its junction with Wardour Street. Founded and run by two Australian wrestlers, Ray Hunter and Paul Lincoln, The 2Is became the launch pad for England's front line of rock and rollers — Cliff Richard, Adam Faith, Marty Wilde and Tommy Steele, all of whom cut their musical teeth in the crowded and smoky confines of the 30 by 10 foot basement club.

Despite skiffle's nationwide appeal it wasn't to everyone's taste. Its primitive instrumentation certainly limited its appeal and the more astute musicians

boards or tea chests to trouble the
e Fifties.

correctly saw it as little more than a fad. *"There will be precious little trade in washboards or tea chests to trouble the second-hand music shops by the end of the Fifties,"* they sagely predicted and they were right, for even though 'Rock Island Line' had been a huge hit, the craze was soon over. The future for these musicians lay in the blues.

It was Cyril Davies who opened Soho's very first blues only club in 1956, specifically to promote black American music. He enlisted the help of fellow blues sympathiser Alexis Korner and together they founded first the Blues & Barrel House Club and, secondly,

England's first real bona fide blues band which they christened Alexis Korner's Breakdown Group before eventually renaming themselves Blues Incorporated.

The Barrel House was located on the first floor of the Roadhouse pub in Wardour Street. By all accounts it was a very low-key affair in its early days, due largely to the minority interest in blues music and the fact that up until then Cyril had run the club as The London Skiffle Centre, which may have put off more discerning enthusiasts. Still, Davies and Korner felt sure that the kind of music they wanted to present would rustle up at least a handful of paying punters per night.

MARQUEE

90 WARDOUR ST.
LONDON, W.1

Friday, June 12th
★ THE YARDBIRDS
★ THE AUTHENTICS

Saturday, June 13th
★ JOE HARRIOTT QUINTET
★ BOBBY BREEN
★ MICHAEL GARRICK TRIO

Sunday, June 14th
JIMMY WITHERSPOON
CHRIS BARBER'S
JAZZ BAND
OTTILIE PATTERSON
JOHNNY TOOGOOD JAZZBAND
Tickets in advance from:
18 Carlisle Street, W.1
Members 6/6   Guests 8/6

Monday, June 15th
★ MANFRED MANN
★ MARK LEEMAN FIVE

Tuesday, June 16th
★ BLUE BEAT
★ DUKE VIN'S SOUND SYSTEM

Wednesday, June 17th
★ HUMPHREY LYTTELTON
AND HIS BAND
★ DENNIS BRAY TRIO

Thursday, June 18th
★ LONG JOHN BALDRY
and the HOOCHIE COOCHIE MEN
with ROD STEWART
★ THE BLUEBIRDS

Fri., Tues., Wed. Members 3/-, Guests 6/-
Mon., Fri. Members 3/-, Guests 7/6
Sat. Members 6/-, Guests 7/6

Blues Incorporated was a fairly experimental affair; an all-acoustic outfit comprising 12-string and six-string guitars, Davies and Korner respectively, Keith Scott on piano, and a bass of the stand-up variety played by Andy Hoogenboom. This was the nucleus around which a floating pool of musicians would take up a nightly guest spot. Usually these were members of the audience, whose numbers were mostly made up of fellow musicians with similar leanings. Korner also played several solo gigs around the area, either fronting or as part of a trio. He appeared mainly at small folk clubs where he found the patrons to be more in tune with his interpretation of the blues. He would play in clubs such as Bunjies in Lichfield Street or The Topic Folk Club at Charing Cross until midnight, then return to The Barrel House to play well in to the early hours with whoever else felt like stepping up

It was with this ad hoc form that Korner and Blues Inc. soldiered on from about 1958 to 1960, building a small but solid following for himself and the band not only in London but outside the capital on their various sojourns out to the provinces. They also earned a well-respected reputation for the club, a reputation good enough to entice some authentic American blues artists in and on to its stage. Artists like Big Bill Broonzy and Otis Spann would turn up unannounced at The Barrel House, intrigued by *"these white kids playing our songs"* and spend the night blowing with Korner, Davies and co, with Broonzy even becoming Korner's house guest for a while.

Of course, genuine blues artists from the US had been visiting England since the early Fifties but only as guests of the touring jazz big bands and only then to play at the many GI hang-outs or air bases, entertaining their boys overseas as it were.

The Barrel House came as something of a shock to the majority of these visiting bluesers, most having only ever experienced playing to black audiences in the US, thanks to America's disgraceful segregation policy which was still very much in place at the end of the Fifties. Yet here they were performing as honoured special guests in an almost exclusively white environment. They were in a club run by musicians for

OTIS SPANN IN LONDON, 1964.

musicians, where black music was revered and those who composed and sang it were given the red carpet treatment and worshipped like gods. The Barrel House would prove to be the single most important link in shaping the beginnings of the British R&B scene, offering our home-grown blues musicians their first ever live experience of the real thing.

Musicians such as Long John Baldry, Geoff Bradford, Brian Knight and Art Wood were just some of the wide-eyed regulars who soaked up the blues at The Barrel House, little realising that they in turn would become equally as influential on the next generation of British R&B musicians.

The next integral link in the development of the music that Mods came to adore was a Muddy Waters-inspired move towards amplification. Davies had grown bored with Blues Incorporated's restrictive acoustic formula and had clubbed together with Korner to buy a tiny 10-watt amplifier, which they could both plug their guitars into and play through. This wasn't a totally new undertaking for Korner. He had messed around with electric guitars before, first in the army and later, at the suggestion of Bill Broonzy, who'd been playing electric guitar for years. It was Broonzy who turned Korner on to the playing styles of Elmore James and Muddy Waters.

Davies was also a fan of Muddy Waters' electric guitar style but he had different ideas as to how the band should sound. Both Davies and Korner wanted to electrify the band but Korner preferred the subtleties of playing acoustically, whereas Davies was absolutely intent on nailing down and reproducing Waters' Chicago blues sound. This was the beginning of the niggling musical difference of opinion that would eventually grow and destroy their partnership. At the time, however, it mattered little because not only did the purchase of that little amp alienate many of the die-hard purists among the Barrel House audience but the landlord himself considered it a purchase too far and promptly sacked them both for being too loud.

Chris Barber hadn't been sitting idle throughout the time Korner and Davies had spent in Blues Incorporated. Far from it. In fact Barber and his band had made a dream trip to America in October 1959 and actually played with Muddy Waters himself at a club deep in the black ghettos of Chicago called Smittys Corner. Like Korner and Davies, Barber had also become obsessed by Waters, so much so that he returned to England vowing to recreate the sounds he had heard using his own band, deep in the heart of Soho. Playing with Waters again a few months later in 1960 only strengthened this resolve and he took his idea to his friend, fellow National Jazz Federation director Harold Pendelton, and his venue, The Marquee, a jazz only club underneath the Academy Cinema in Oxford Street.

Barber told Pendelton his idea for bringing Chicago blues to London by using the old trick of slipping in a different section of music during the interval section of his own band. This time it would be a blues set instead of skiffle and the band would be fronted by a vocalist, the female blues singer Ottilie Paterson. Although obviously not convinced, Pendleton generously gave his friend the dead Wednesday night slot in order to put his plan in to action. Barber approached Korner and the latter agreed to help flesh out Barber's sound. The sessions went well and Barber felt confident enough to tour the band. They even sat in as backing band for Muddy Waters' harmonica player Jimmy Cotton on his solo trip to London and cut a two-EP set with the harp player. Despite this and the fact that the band was pretty much in regular live work throughout 1960/61, mainstream acceptance still eluded the blues.

Despite the efforts of Korner, Davies and Barber, concert promoters in Britain were still reluctant to accept blues, let alone electric blues, as a popular form of music that could replace jazz. Some support came in 1961, when a small article in *Jazz News* stated that *"it applauded the Barber Band for moving away from the strict confines of trad jazz"* and that *"the band's latest and perhaps biggest single step forward stride has been the inclusion of Alexis Korner, whose switch to amplified guitar has bleached the hair of some of the purists and ethinicians."*

This limited critical success, combined with Korner's frustration with only being able to play small sets of blues with Barber's Band, encouraged the guitarist to reform Blues Incorporated, but to do this he would need the back up of Cyril Davies.

Alexis hadn't had much contact with Davies since the pair's dismissal from The Barrel House, but he felt sure the guitarist would be keen to form a permanent electric guitar-based blues band, which of course he was. As it happened Davies had by now all but abandoned his guitar in favour of the harmonica. This didn't phase Korner, who hoped the switch would eliminate the sort of musical disagreements that had dogged their earlier collaboration. He even wrote an article for *Jazz News* in a bid to encourage Cyril's new direction, citing the importance of the harmonica in blues music.

In the piece Korner said: *"There was a time when the harmonica was very popular. It was cheap, compact and portable. It was in fact ideal for the home music maker. It was the diatonic harmonica, the common mouth organ which was really popular.*

"The ordinary suck and blow instrument was ideally suited to the blues. The sound was more intense, a better match than the more expensive chromatic version for the incisive tones for jug bands and country blues singers.

"In the hands of a good player, the harmonica could produce an astoundingly wide range of dynamics and tone colour. One has but to hear recordings by Noah Lewis, Will Shade, Sonny Terry, Sonny Boy Williamson and Little Walter to realise how personally different each of these players makes his harmonica sound."

Alexis went on to explain just how Sonny Boy Williamson had brought about such a shift in blues music and announced that the era of the blue harp hero was now upon us. It's important to remember that this article appeared in the paper long before The Beatles released their harmonica-led debut single 'Love Me Do' or the Stones their equally harp-heavy 'Come On'.

The R&B Show
CITY HALL (OVAL HALL)

THE ROLLING STONES
The Big 3
WAYNE FONTANA and the MINDBENDERS

The Sheffields

Johnny Tempest and the CADILLACS

VANCE ARNOLD AND THE AVENGERS

The VANTENNAS

KAREN YOUNG

The 4 PLUS 1

WEDNESDAY 13th NOV.

Compered by the STRINGFELLOW BROS.

Tickets 4/- 5/- 6/-

from Wilson Peck * Black Cat Club or Blue Moon Club.

Discussions were held between Barber, Pendleton, Korner and Davies and it was agreed that the new band would do the entire interval slot in its own right, starting on January 3, 1962.

So it was that Blues Incorporated returned to the West End and played their first successful night at The Marquee. These gigs lasted mere weeks, for no sooner had the interval slots commenced than their sudden popularity became an instant problem for everyone concerned. Korner and Davies wanted to play longer sets and would often do so, while Barber felt his own good nature was being taken advantage of and his own audience compromised.

The only solution was for Blues Incorporated to quit The Marquee and find a club of their own. The search took the band to Ealing and to a venue frequented by the group's new vocalist, Art Wood.

Art Wood: *"It was 1962 by then and I remember I was going up the Uxbridge Road for what seemed like the ten thousandth time on my Vespa 125, which incidentally cost me one hundred and twenty-five quid which always struck me as funny, one pound per square inch.*

"I was going to a little place called the Barasque Club which was a little underground drinking club, opposite Ealing Broadway tube station. Now when I say underground I don't mean it was an illicit, word-of-mouth, in-the-know type, cool, hip place, I mean it was just held underground, in the basement of a little ABC tea shop. Little jazz bands had always played there in the evenings and it was still popular with what was the tail end, the thin tail end of the beatniks-come-skiffle crowd which my brother Ted was into, with his band 'The Original London Skiffle Group'. It was right on the cusp of Mod, the very early ones. The club's owner renamed it on the live music nights 'The Moist Hoist' on the account of there being no ventilation, so the condensation would literally run down the walls so much they had to erect a tarpaulin canopy over the stage to stop the bands getting soaked from the dripping ceiling. I told the owner about how popular the blues was and I convinced him that he needed Alexis and his band down at his club and he went for it.

"I went back and told Alexis and Cyril and arranged for us all to go back down together and give it the once over. I remember I picked them both up in Wardour Street on an Aerial Hunt Master 650 motor bike, because it had a side car — I didn't have a car. It wasn't Mod, but it got all three of us there. And they both loved it. They renamed it the very imaginative Ealing Club."

The Ealing Club opened on March 17, 1962. Alexis and Cyril continued with the winning formula they'd honed at The Barrel House, inviting guest stars, fellow musicians or members of the audience up on stage to jam with the band. Only this time it was different. Within a few short weeks of relocating to the suburbs, the band noticed that their audience had started to change.

Their pioneering hard work on behalf of the blues had paid off. Word had spread across London and the group found that they were playing to a completely new generation of kids

This generation had been too young for jazz or skiffle and yet they hated the watered-down style of rock'n'roll currently on offer from Brit rockers such as Cliff Richard. These kids wanted a scene of their own. They were receptive to the blues, or rather to rhythm & blues, and they seemed to understand exactly what the likes of Korner and Davies were trying to achieve.

THE BLACK MARKET

By 1964 the rhythm & blues scene had completely revitalised the entire club scene in south-west London, from Ealing to Shepherds Bush, down Oxford Street, and back to Soho. Almost every club had gone over to R&B and all were reporting record-breaking business.

The Marquee had even started to announce over the PA just how many people were in the club each night. *"Ladies and gentlemen, tonight an all-time record, there are 874 of us in here."* Just up the road, The 100 Club had forgone its jazz only policy and was now featuring resident R&B favourites, The Art Woods.

Crowds at The Scene club in Ham Yard were at maximum capacity for an up-and-coming outfit from Shepherds Bush who called themselves The High Numbers. Meanwhile, The Flamingo had gone from strength to strength, thanks to the club's resident band, Georgie Fame and His Blue Flames.

The band had made their name as the permanent fixture at the famous Flamingo allnighters. Fame himself was a jazz-influenced organ player whose style was described as a cross between Booker T. and Jimmy Smith, while his band was a dual saxophone-led R&B powerhouse. Their repertoire was cobbled together from hundreds of records given to the band by The Flamingo's large GI and West Indian contingent. Rare and obscure records by Eddie Jefferson, Jimmy Witherspoon, Jimmy Reed and King Pleasure were regularly covered by Fame and his band. As a result they became a 'must see' Mod favourite.

The West Indian faction among the band's following were responsible for the massive popularity of a club in Carnaby Street called The Roaring Twenties. This was specifically a black club and when it opened in 1961 it became the first London venue to play ska and blue-beat music. Its clientele were also responsible for the particularly West Indian-influenced style of dressing known as the rude boy look — pork pie hats (a flat-topped, small-brimmed variation on the bowler), braces and tassled loafers worn with white socks.

Mods would go to the club on weekends, pick up dance and clothes tips and hopefully score drugs such as marijuana, hemp or pills. As the young Mod who was the subject of Len Deighton's 'Dossier of London' tactfully said: *"At the moment we're hero worshipping the spades — they can dance and sing. The more sophisticated teenagers can go to spade clubs in the West End. They're family clubs really, women take kids along, they're not really teenage clubs. You can take hashish and hemp, inject into the veins. It makes you feel wonderful, it's a sort of inward thing, you don't do anything. You just feel fantastic, we do the shake and hitch-hike to fast numbers but we're going back to dancing close because the spades do it. We have to get all our clothes made because as soon as anything is in the shops it becomes too common. I once went to the West Indian Club, where everyone made their own clothes. It was fantastic, everyone was individual, everyone was showing themselves as they really wanted to be."*

Ken Browne: *"I think the Wembley Mods were fairly well known at the time, wherever we went. It was a fairly Mod area, White City. All the East London guys were fairly hard. We avoided them when we used to go into town to Tiles or The Roaring Twenties. There was always a definite East London contingent there that we avoided. There were always a lot of blacks at those clubs, they had really moved in on the scene. They used to wear mohair suits. There were two black guys in particular, one was called Cherry and the other one was called Glossy. Fairly racist these days, I know, but that was their nicknames and they used to answer to them. They used to wear suits, maroon leathers and (carry) rolled-up umbrellas. In a fight they would bash people with their brollies. It was quite amazing, you could take these big umbrellas on to the dance floor, if you could call it a dance floor. There was a fight every week. Somebody would wade in with a knife or a brolly with a sharpened tip but I never saw anyone get glassed. It was mainly fisticuffs and it would be over in seconds and that would be it for another week. There were bouncers but they were big old boys and a bit slow off the mark."*

It wasn't only live music venues that attracted large Mod crowds; discos were also incredibly popular. These included clubs such as The Scene which opened in 1963, taking over the old Cy Laurie jazz club premises in Gt. Windmill Street, and boasting London's top DJ in a character called Guy Stevens. The latter was said to be the owner of the greatest collection of American black, soul, blues and R&B records anywhere in the country, courtesy once again of the enterprising GIs who did a fair trade in precious vinyl.

Ken Browne: *"I knew a guy who paid one GI a week's wages for 'You Better Move On' by Arthur Alexander and the very next week the same guy came back with about half a dozen of 'em. We took the piss out of our mate and he just said, 'You can take the piss out of me, mate, but I had that record a week ago.' We thought the GIs were loaded but they were mostly poor black conscripts but sharp as a knife."*

La Discotheque, in Wardour Street, was probably the first club to play only recorded music in London. The Ad Lib in Leicester Square and Annabels in Berkeley Square were also 'in' places. However, these clubs and others, such as the Scotch of St. James in Masons Yard, Dollys in Jermyn Street and for a short time the Cromwellian on the Cromwell Road, were for expensive nights out favoured by the slightly older and predominantly better off Mods.

Ken Browne: *"You would also get them in Tiles, the upper-class kids. They had the moves and they could afford to dress a bit better. They used all those clubs, The Scotch and Cromwellian, the average Mod didn't. I'd never have got in. It was also about seven quid to get in or something ridiculous which was unbelievable in those days. There was a whole different scene going on in those places."*

In October 1962, *Melody Maker* ran the news item that Alexis Korner was adding a Hammond organ player to his Blues Incorporated line-up in the shape of Graham Bond, and that Cyril Davies was quitting to form his own harp-driven solo outfit, 'The Cyril Davies All Stars'.

Art Wood: *"I'd been fired by now and had formed The Artwoods. Cyril had hated the way the band was going, hated saxophones, hated Alexis and would never have had a Hammond player in. Cyril got Alexis to fire me. I was getting less and less singing time anyway, so it wasn't a problem. I knew it was coming, Alexis used to come round my house with the set of songs I would do the following night and suddenly he stopped coming. Mick was doing more gigs than me, until he joined the Stones, so it was all a bit up in the air because there wasn't a fixed line-up. Alexis told me, 'Cyril told me to fire you because he thinks you're not nasty enough to be a blues singer.' I asked him 'How do I become nasty then?' and he said, 'You can't, you're not spiteful enough.' Cyril was like that, I remember Mick asking Cyril how to bend notes and Cyril just said, 'Get a fucking pair of pliers.' He was nice like that. He wanted his own band and that was that. The All Stars."*

The All Stars would feature the vocal talents of Long John Baldry, a singer whose reputation had grown mainly on the Continent, Germany in particular. Baldry returned, courtesy of a plane ticket bought for him by Korner who had actually lined up the singer for his own band, only to be told Baldry had made his decision after literally tossing a coin. London now had two top-class blues acts vying for the still growing R&B fan base.

Richard Barnes: *"The first time I'd seen the Cyril Davies All Stars was when Baldry was singing with them at The Railway Hotel in Richmond. Just before the crowds got really huge and the club moved to the football ground. It was the first R&B club I ever went to. I later ran the club and put The High Numbers in as the resident band. It was the most important club for Mods outside the West End.*

"Baldry was this unbelievably clean-cut Mod, six foot seven inches tall in a suit, with an elephant collar shirt. He had all the gear from playing in Europe.

"He would hang about with Rod Stewart who was a real show-off Mod, but he also got a lot from Baldry. I remember seeing Rod and he had the first backcombed bouffant haircut I'd ever seen. It must have stood up six inches at the back. Baldry was gay and Rod used to camp it up very convincingly. I was sure he was gay in

those days. I know he turned out to be the real geezer with birds on both arms but back then I wasn't convinced.

"Anyway, Baldry, I remember, absolutely detested Davies, they were poles apart. Davies was this old balding guy (Davies was only in his early thirties) who worked on the railways during the day. Scruffy old trousers and always drunk.

"One night Cyril had got blind drunk and had fallen down asleep at the side of the stage, and Baldry was kicking him saying 'You old cunt.' I went off Baldry after that but it worked for a little while and seeing Cyril Davies was a turning point for me. He got me interested in R&B and from his audience at the Crawdaddy/ Richmond club, I became aware of Mods."

Cyril Davies' All Stars was to be a tragically short-lived affair, releasing only two singles on the Pye label, 'Country Line Special' and 'Preaching The Blues'. Davies died aged 32 of a pneumonia-related heart attack after waiting in the rain for hours following a gig on January 7, 1964.

FACES WITHOUT SHADOWS
AN INTERVIEW WITH MARK FELD (MARC BOLAN),
TOWN MAGAZINE, 1962

Mark Feld, Peter Sugar and Michael Simmonds were brought up in Stoke Newington. The most important thing in the world to them is their clothes: they have cupboards and shelves bulging with suits and shirts often designed by themselves in bright, strange and violent colours. In their vocabulary they, and the few other contemporaries of whom they approve, are described as 'faces' — the necessary ingredients are youth, a sharp eye for dressing, and a general lack of mercy towards the rest of the world.

Feld is 15 years old, and still at school. His family has just moved from Stamford Hill to a pre-fab out in Wimbledon. Of this he does not approve. The queues of Teds outside the cinemas in Wimbledon look just like a contest for the worst haircut, he says. At least the boys of old Stamford Hill dress sharply, and who would want a new, clean house if it is in unsympathetic surroundings?

Nonetheless cleanliness is of vital importance to him. Shining with soap and health, he is apparently tireless and often goes for days on end without any sleep; there is never a trace of fatigue or boredom in his face. What is the point of all this energy and all the soap and water? Where is the goal towards which he is obviously running as fast as his impeccably shod feet can carry him? It is nowhere. He is running to stay in the same place, and he knows that by the time he has reached his mid-twenties the exhausting race will be over and he will have lost. Living for the present is a mild way of putting it: for him and for all the other sharp young faces the present is so short and so intensely satisfying that they cannot give even a minute of their time to considering the future.

Leading this sort of life develops arrogance. It is naturally assumed that all girls must fall headlong in love when they meet a face; those that are not pretty enough or who fail to come up to scratch in some way are referred to as maggots by the boys, and roundly insulted whenever they appear. Perhaps the girls are really quite glad that some square and ordinary young

men exist — a world peopled entirely by faces would be a nightmare.

Mark is the most remarkable of the three because he is five years younger than either of the other two and appears to have no visible means of support. His father is a lorry driver and his mother works in Berwick Market: she is joined there by her son on Saturdays when he puts in a full day's work. Otherwise the week is his to bend and stretch to his will, extending the days into the nights and telescoping the deadly Sundays into a brief sleep. In common with the others his conversation only becomes animated when asked about his clothes. He says, 'I've got ten suits, eight sports jackets, fifteen pairs of slacks, thirty to thirty-five good shirts, about twenty jumpers, three leather jackets, two suede jackets, five or six pairs of shoes and thirty exceptionally good ties.'

Peter Sugar has a Polish father and a sister who owns a hairdressing salon in Hornsey, where he works as her assistant. 'I'm 20 and I take home about £12 a week. Sometimes a bit more. I give my mum 50s a week and the rest is mine. Most of it goes on clothes. Clothes and taxis.'

Both he and Michael Simmonds, who also works at hairdressing in the New North Road, have been cutting each other's hair for years and joke about their work a good deal. 'I sent two women out today the same colour as they came in' (this must be largely the woman's fault if she can't tell the colour of her own hair), 'and I've got varicose veins already from standing all day long.'

Sugar is definitely the leader of the group. As none of them has a car it's he who organises lifts from acquaintances on their complicated cross-London evenings. Once used, the hapless owner of the car will be lucky if he is allowed to join the party or stay with the boys at all; he is simply made into a convenience and then forgotten.

Michael Simmonds is the quietest and most reflective and has some regularity in his life: every Friday night he has supper with his aunt and sets her hair for her afterwards. He is strongly influenced by Peter, who likes to be the spokesman on every possible occasion, but he is prepared to reveal that he, like the others, has no

ambitions whatsoever. 'I'd like to travel, maybe go to Africa' is all he will say.

The parents seem to be unaffected by their lack of control over the children. Perhaps it was their initial lack of interest that caused them to be as they are, but the present situation is summed up by Mark Feld's mother. 'He irons his shirts himself. I can't do them half as well.'

'You've got to be different from the other kids,' says Feld. 'I mean you got to be two steps ahead. The stuff that half the haddocks you see around are wearing I was wearing years ago. A kid in my class came up to me in his new suit, an Italian box it was, he says "Just look at the length of your jacket," he says. "You're not with it," he says.'"I was wearing that style two years ago," I said. Of course they don't like that. Not many of them like me much at our school, especially the masters — but they leave me alone now. If it's football or anything — I mean that's not my style at all — they say "Oh never mind about Feld", and I go and sunbathe or something.'

'It's getting harder to be different now,' says Simmonds, the quiet one.

'Yeah,' says Feld. 'Remember three years ago, it was easy then. We used to go round on scooters in Levi's and leather jackets. It was a lot easier then.'

But three years ago he would only be 12. 'That's right,' says Feld.

'Half the tailors you go to just don't want to know' says Sugar. 'You got to tell them exactly what you want and they say yes, yes, yes, they know, they know what the styles are, all the kids go to them and then they produce a monstrosity with a little box jacket and vents and covered buttons and you just can't wear it.'

'You have to leave a small deposit,' says Simmonds. 'And then if you don't like the result you don't collect. I done that lots of times. I mean you have to.'

Sugar says: 'Bilgorri in Bishopsgate — he's a great tailor. He'll make exactly what you want. It's a real haddocky-looking place he has but he does what you want. All the faces go to Bilgorri. And John Stevens. He's very good on trousers. Hardly any place in London makes good trousers. They're all baggy here.' He tugs at the seat of his own trousers. Barely an eighth of an inch comes away.

'They aren't good on shoulders either,' says Feld. 'They can't make good shoulders like those French shoulders. I brought a jacket back from Paris — I was in Paris with my parents but I didn't like it much — and this jacket was just rubbish over there but it's great here. Great shoulders.'

'We've all had suits from Burtons,' says Sugar.

'We have, I admit it. You take a bit of a chance with Burtons but if you tell them exactly what you want you can get a good suit.'

'C & A suits are good, too,' says Feld. 'You have to look at them all and try them on but we've all found a suit we liked there.'

'You found that sort of mohair one, didn't you Michael?' said Sugar. 'And I found that tweed one. Just the thing for point-to-points.' Pause.

'I'm a Conservative,' said Sugar. 'I mean Conservatives are for the rich, aren't they, and everyone wants to be rich, really, don't they.'

'They've been in a long time and they done all right,' said Simmonds.

'Yeah, like he says, they're for the rich, really, so I'm for them,' says Feld.

'Of course I don't know much about it,' says Sugar.

'The Ban the Bomb lot are dead right and everything but I wouldn't march or anything,' says Simmonds.

'It's all exhibitionist isn't it?' says Feld. 'I'm all for that. I mean I'm all for anyone who's exhibitionist. You don't just want to be like everyone else. You got to be different.'

Pause.

'I read a good book the other day,' says Feld. 'The Life of Beau Brummel. He was just like us really. You know, came up from nothing. Then he met Royalty and got to know all the big blokes and he had a lot of clothes. He came to nothing in the end through gambling. I don't gamble.'

'I don't read much,' said Simmonds.

'We used to gamble a bit, though, didn't we Michael?' says Sugar. 'Chemmy and those things. We knew this friend of ours who had a club and we used to go there. We've stopped going now.'

'The place we go now is the Discotheque in Wardour Street,' says Feld.

'All the faces go there,' says Sugar. 'You can dance and get soft drinks. Faces like us don't drink except wine. We like wine. A glass of beer in one hand and a cheese sandwich in the other's not our style at all.'

'We've been to the Establishment a few times,' says Simmonds. 'You hang around outside and join on the end when a crowd's going in.'

'Then you stand in the bar among all the faces as if you own the place and everyone looks at you and wonders who you are,' says Sugar.

'They wonder if you're a playboy or something,' says Feld.

Pause.

'We've tried to get into the Saddle Room,' says Sugar. 'We've tried a few times. But they won't let us in. Still. No harm in trying.'

Pause.

'You can get some things very cheap if you keep your eyes open,' says Sugar. 'I mean look at those new C & A shirts. Only 14s 6d. Some faces won't look at them because they're only 14s 6d. That's just ridiculous.'

'And that gingham shirt in Woolworths this morning,' says Feld. 'Only ten bob. A few alterations and it would look as good as a four guinea job from John Michael.'

'We bought these stick pins from Woolworths this morning,' says Sugar. 'Only 3d each. They are really women's hat pins but you can't tell can you? We've got pearl ones and gold ones and black ones and we can ring the changes.'

'You have to watch them, though,' says Feld.

'They work up a bit if you don't watch them.'

Pause for adjustment of stick pins.

'These shoes cost 7 gns in Pinnays in Bond Street,' says Feld. 'I think if you pay a bit extra for shoes they last longer.'

Pause.

'We're all a bit exhibitionist,' says Sugar. 'I admit. Some of our clothes are a bit effeminate but they have to be. I mean you have to be a bit camp. I mean who cares.'

'You get a lot of jeers and shouts round our way,' says Feld. 'If you wear something that's a bit different it's "Nancy" and "Look at that queer".'

'We're not, so who cares,' says Sugar.

'But you get into fights over it all the time, anyway,' says Feld.

'We don't look for them. We're not the type,' says Simmonds.

'Just a bit ago me and Michael were at this dance hall in Hackney,' says Sugar. 'We twist a lot. We were twisting two years ago and it used to cause such a lot of trouble that we were told to stop it. Nowadays everyone twists so we have to have a different twist. I mean there's the straight twist and the rock twist and the sophisticated twist, you have to be different. Anyway this lad at Hackney, he'd been drinking a bit and he grabbed me by the lapels and said "I hear you been looking for me to sort me out". I said I'd never see him before and was turning away when he come in with his nut. So I started in and Michael came in and his mates came in and it was murder. I wouldn't care if they was my size, but they're always enormous. I mean that one that hit you, Michael, he must have had a fist that size.'

'Yeah,' said Simmonds, remembering.

'I went to the Calypso hall over Croydon way,' says Feld. 'I was wearing a pair of white cotton trousers and a suede jacket. Well, there was a big line of Teds there. You should have heard them when they saw me. Whistling, shouting, laughing. I had to walk all the way past them.'

A short silence for brooding.

'It's because we're different,' says Sugar.

'Anything different they just hit out,' says Feld. 'There's no arguing or settling it with talk, it's just hit out.'

Another pause.

'What I want is to make money and do just what I like,' says Sugar. 'That's what I want to do. Just what I like. Trouble is I'm lazy. Frankly, mind you, I work hard.'

'John Stevens, now,' says Feld. 'You got to hand it to him. All those shops and he's still only 26 or something. You got to hand it to him.'

'And that face that does the laundrettes,' says Sugar. 'Only thirty something and he's a millionaire.'

'And blokes like Cliff Richard and Adam Faith,' says Feld. 'I mean, I suppose they're had-its in a way but they've done something.'

'They've made their way at something.'

'And Elvis Presley...'

'And Frank Sinatra...'

'And Albert Finney...'

Pause.

'Remember those winkle-pickers we used to wear from Stan's?' says Feld.

They fall about with laughter.

'Those days it was easy to be different,' says Sugar.

'Harder now,' says Feld.

'Definitely,' says Simmonds.

GONE TO TOWN
All dressed up with somewhere to go...

The now-famous *Town* magazine article was the first known public acknowledgement of Mods in the press. It featured an eight-page photo spread and an interview with, among others, a 15-year-old kid called Mark Feld who would become better known when he changed his name to Marc Bolan.

In the article Feld talked about the price of clothes, about finding the right tailors and about how the need to be inventive was of crucial importance to dressing the part of a Mod. The article was also the first time the phrase 'face' appeared in print.

This was confirmation that by 1962 the whole movement had developed to the extent that it had its own vocabulary. Before this article appeared, the only people that knew about Mods were the Mods themselves. This low profile can be attributed largely to the fact that unlike the Teds before them, there wasn't a specific look to identify a Mod in the street. Up until then Mods had been largely isolated from each other; just little pockets of like-minded people who, unbeknownst to one another, had the same interests in common, the same clothes and music. The Mods weren't a gang or a group or a tribe or whatever collective term had been used before to describe a style movement. They were individual people who were clothes obsessive and fashion conscious. Above all else they had the same attitude to life.

The Teddy boys of the Fifties had shown the way, making it acceptable for young working-class males to make-up and dress up. Before them there was no discernable difference in the style of clothes available across the entire age span.

Casual clothes or fun clothes existed only in the movies. If you were young and British you dressed like your mum or dad. In the Fifties the idea that Britain could one day be a fashion leader was as laughable as, well, landing a man on the moon.

The only problem with the Teds was that while inventing the generation gap and the teenager, they'd forgotten completely about individualism. All Teds looked the same. They created a look that was so precise, it became little more than a uniform.

Mods didn't have a uniform. They were mostly male, vain, snobbish and predominantly working class. Many early Mods were Jews whose parents worked in the rag trade where, presumably, the clothes fetish started. They had more money than any previous generation and yet worked considerably less.

Johnny Moke *"There were a lot of Jewish tailors, I was getting my suits made by tailors when I was 13. I used to hang out with Marc Bolan in Stamford Hill when he was about 16. It progressed very slowly to begin with, in fact it didn't progress, it evolved. It would go from someone making a small choice in maybe a collar, which made it slightly exaggerated. Every week or every month it would progress in that way. It was never drastic to start with, it certainly wasn't as drastic as things come and go now, it was evolution."*

Paul Stagg: *"We were definitely the first generation to have money to spend on ourselves on clothes and records or frivolity. The whole record industry as we know it today evolved from our generation. It was hardly an industry before. It was Max Bygraves.*

"Music only got a life in the early Fifties the same as teenagers. Of course, the Teds came first but they were really young adults but not really teenagers in my eyes.

"I also think ours was the first generation that hadn't been obsessed by the war, we were in a way selfish in that respect. It didn't matter to us at all, yet I looked at my older brothers and they were all fucking shell-shocked — they knew their place, we didn't give a shit.

"We were the first to miss out on national service. We just missed it, even the Teds got caught up in that one. What happened to them was, they were young, out and about and enjoying themselves when bang, call up. They came out a grown-up at 20, a fucking grown-up at 20. Mods never grew up and I still don't think they have, they're all still 18 at heart."

They were a new breed all right, teenage dandies reacting against all that had come before — the Fifties yobbos and, even worse, the scruffy, cider-drinking ex-students who grew beards, worse loose sweaters and liked watered-down British trad jazz.

Mods identified only with what was new, sophisticated and clean. Although there were only handfuls of Mods to begin with, they all gravitated to the same places: the coffee bars in Soho. There, they would meet, talk and pick up ideas for clothes, or simply admire each others' look. It was narcissistic, self-absorbed and even downright effeminate.

Ken Browne: *"There was a definite gay influence involved with the early Mods. The London clubs would have a lot of gays in them wearing outrageous white suits with big high heels. Mods took that influence, it became a case of looking as pretty as possible, as nice as possible.*

"I never knew any gay Mods. Every single one I met was very heterosexual, even though they weren't that interested in girls. They were so wrapped up in themselves, interested in their scooters, clothes and pills. I had a few girlfriends but on the whole they weren't into the scene. The clubs were just full of blokes."

Slowly this narcissism and obsessiveness over clothes spread to others. What had once been a expression of individualism became a genuine cult.

Ken Browne: *"Suits were always bought made to measure, so each time a Mod had one made he varied it a little. A different, little touch, like covered buttons, the box jacket would have side vents, one, two or three inches long or the cuffs would be open with a link button or a butterfly cuff. Some jackets were cut rounded at the bottom like a Spanish bolero jacket. The trousers varied a lot, stepped bottoms, which were cut, back to the seams, so the front was higher than the back, resting on the shoe at the front and covering the back, buttons were sewn on the seams, they were nearly always straight legged though.*

"The suits were always dark navy blue, or black. We found this black guy who used to make suits for all the cool blacks at The Roaring Twenties, 'Newmans' on the North End Road, off Norfolk Road. He also did shirts with what were called 'Billy Eckstine' collars which were a roll collar. No buttons, like a roll neck jumper, the Italians had a modified version of that so we would go to Newmans and get these nice roll collar shirts made. We used to walk around Soho and see Italian waiters in their civvies and they had obviously bought their suits from Italy and they looked wonderful. The trousers always had a four-inch inside turn-up to get the trouser to hang beautifully and there would be a lovely little stitch line.

"Plain colours were later replaced by the checks, Prince of Wales check, black watch trousers. Prince of Wales was always very dear."

They were so wrapped up in themse
clothes and pills. The clubs were just

interested in their scooters,
f blokes...

Mods have been constantly
but it was more of a working

"The jackets were all waisted. This meant they had two seams at the side and one in the centre so that you could have a centre vent, as opposed to two side vents.

"The two side vents were gone by the mid-Sixties. It started at nine inches then it went to 12 inches and then it got out of hand with some guys having 18 inches. So you would have a longer jacket made so you could have a 22-inch vent. Mods would actually say 'How long is your vent? Eighteen? I've got 22.' You would have to have the longest vent possible, almost like a status symbol. It was very easy to go too far. I had three suits which is nothing these days but the Sixties was a different world. Young guys these days have thousands of pounds worth of clothes but coming out of the Fifties, everything was austere. If your dad had one suit, he was lucky. Mods, although it's true, did have more money than kids had ever done before, they were still on the whole, very working class.

"This was certainly true, when the whole thing got really big. Most Mods came from very impoverished backgrounds.

"Mods have been constantly described as a working-class phenomenon but it was more of a working-class reaction against authority, a street level rebellion that was expressed by looking far smarter, harder and cleaner than your so-called betters or elders.

"OK so this was a bit of a sham as the first part was only (predominantly) made possible by hire purchase, clothes made and bought on the never-never.

"I remember the average debt was around the £200 mark. I had a Saturday job which paid about seventeen and six, not even a £1, about 75p working in a toy shop in Wembley High Street. My mates were all doing grocery jobs or something which paid £1 or £2 and that was your lot. You had to go out and buy clothes and have fun with that at the weekend. I remember The Starlight Ballroom was one and nine to get in and a pint of bitter was two bob, so that was your seventeen and six gone. Eight pints of bitter and your entrance fee".

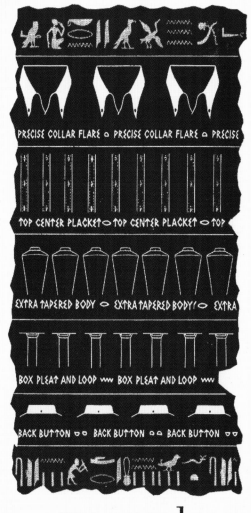

bed as a working-class phenomenon
reaction against authority.

A short half-parting across the centre o
opposite directions, away from the parti
of having a two-tiered head.

Mod haircuts were crucially important to the look and surprisingly difficult to obtain. There were no hair stylists for men in the early Sixties, only old-style barbers who simply cut hair short. The haircuts never had names, nor were they based around any particular fashions. The Teds had made some headway in the late Fifties with their variation on an Elvis/Jerry Lee Lewis theme, charmingly referred to as a D.A. or Duck's Arse which was a wild, greased-up creation that from the back that looked exactly like... well, a duck's arse.

The Mods didn't want grease, oil or lotions. They preferred a dry, natural look which for the most part confused the British barbers who were used to rubbing copious amounts of foul-smelling goo into customers' scalps. Backcombing was probably the most flamboyant and feminine of hairstyles that the Mods toyed with. A short half-parting across the centre of the head with the hair combed in opposite directions, away from the parting. This gave the wearer the appearance of having a two-tiered head. This style was taken to ridiculous lengths by Steve Marriott and Roger Daltrey but by far the worst offenders were Mick from Dave Dee, Dozy, Beaky Mick and Tich fame and Rod Stewart in his Rod the Mod guise. Johnny Moke was another who favoured the backcombed barnet: *"We thought it was a very French look although I'm sure it wasn't."* Eventually the traditional barbers caught up with the styles the Mods wanted but on the whole Mods went to ladies' hair salons for their cuts.

Graham Hughes: *"Haircuts moved away from the razor cuts and got longer. Haircuts got longer after Warren Beatty's first film, in fact. He played this bloke who was into his girlfriend's mother and that set a new precedent. 'Can you take me home to meet your mum?' He had longer hair in it, a longer, softer look. Girls used to say they liked putting their hands through your hair and all that. We stopped going to the place we had gone to for years after that, it was OK to let your girlfriend cut it".*

As Mods and Mod styles grew, the suited look began to merge with the more casual street, or everyday wear. Cycling clothes had caught on and were worn with other sports accessories like bowling shoes, cycling or running shoes (with the spike removed). Hush Puppies were the favourite Mod shoes and the favourite Hush Puppies were Clarks' desert boots. These were worn with polo shirts, T-shirts or sweat shirts.

Johnny Moke: *"I bought my first pair of Densons in 1958 and after that I started buying my shoes from Stan's of Battersea or Raoul in Wardour Street. Shirts were still Austins in Shaftesbury Avenue which was much better than Brookes Brothers, more adventurous than Brookes. They were about two guineas each. Levi's were that much as well, they eventually imported them. There was a shop on Kings Road that started to import them and another one in Kingston which was a shop that imported all sorts of American clothes. It was like a hardware shop, I think it was called Brandos and it sold overalls and dungarees, work clothes and Levi's. It wasn't a fashion shop at all."*

Paul Stagg: *"Soho was run by the Italians. Italy first, then Malta, then Soho. There were the Greeks and that's where a big influence on shoes came from. The Greeks made beautiful shoes. First came the really long points 'Stan's Georgious', which were really long so we had to be inventive. We would spend all day at college, designing different shorter points and where the buckle was going to be.*

"Then a shorter point would come out so you'd think, 'I'll stop that then, and do a rounder point' and you would have to find someone to make them because you couldn't buy them. We found this bloke in Drummond Street, off Euston Road. A guy called Sulky and he could make fantastic shoes for twelve quid. All made to last, handmade leather shoes with a Louis XIV heel, made from our designs.

"Mods were short, on the whole. All the Mods from the East End were very short people and the Italians

head with the hair combed in
is gave the wearer the appearance

BELL BOTTON

The Jeans b
Weg's Texa

MADE IN
SINGAPORE

Size : 38

Waist : 76

Inseam : 81

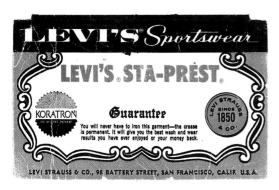

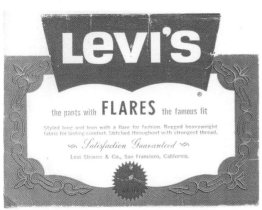

PERMANENTLY PRESSED - NEVER NEEDS IRONING

were short as well. So the boots would have a stack heel. Almost slightly cowboyish. It would give height and allow the trouser to hang better.

"It sounds like we were all little rich boys but it was only because you couldn't buy the clothes we wanted. We couldn't afford it and we were forever in debt.

"The only thing we bought were the plastic macs from C & As. Nylon or plastic macs. Cecil Gees sold the genuine article. It was an old Italian man's style. They would wear them over their suits on a scooter and this caught on really quick and became part of a uniform with Mods, which started to defeat the object of being different. They came with a little nylon cap in the pocket and from this we went back to the cycling beret. We were constantly having to be more and more resourceful.

"I can't emphasise enough just how difficult it was to find the right sort of clothes and just how important and exciting Carnaby Street was. It's especially hard to appreciate this when you look at it nowadays. We couldn't buy what we wanted, not just shoes. I had to change jackets, take buttons off. I remember I couldn't buy a blazer anywhere that was the right shape. I had to go to a second-hand shop and buy an old blazer and waist it so that it was the right shape. Upstairs in Moss Bros there was a room where you could buy second-hand Moss Bros suits and great big second-hand overcoats. Great big double-breasted overcoats and we would get them to take the shoulder pads out so that they had this natural Italian shoulder, which was a softer look, rather than that English look, which was a military look. Take the shoulder pads out and shorten the sleeves and you would have the look as best you could.

"If you relayed this to kids today, they wouldn't believe it. Kids today worry where they're going to get their drugs from, we worried where we would get our clothes from. Not even if we could afford them, simply where to get them from."

The humble sweat shirt was another unbelievably difficult item of clothing to find in the early Sixties and custom-made ones started their own (small) fashion revolution. The trend started following the first British invasion of groups to America, when visiting bands were given promotional sweat shirts from the US radio stations they called in on. Those bands would then wear

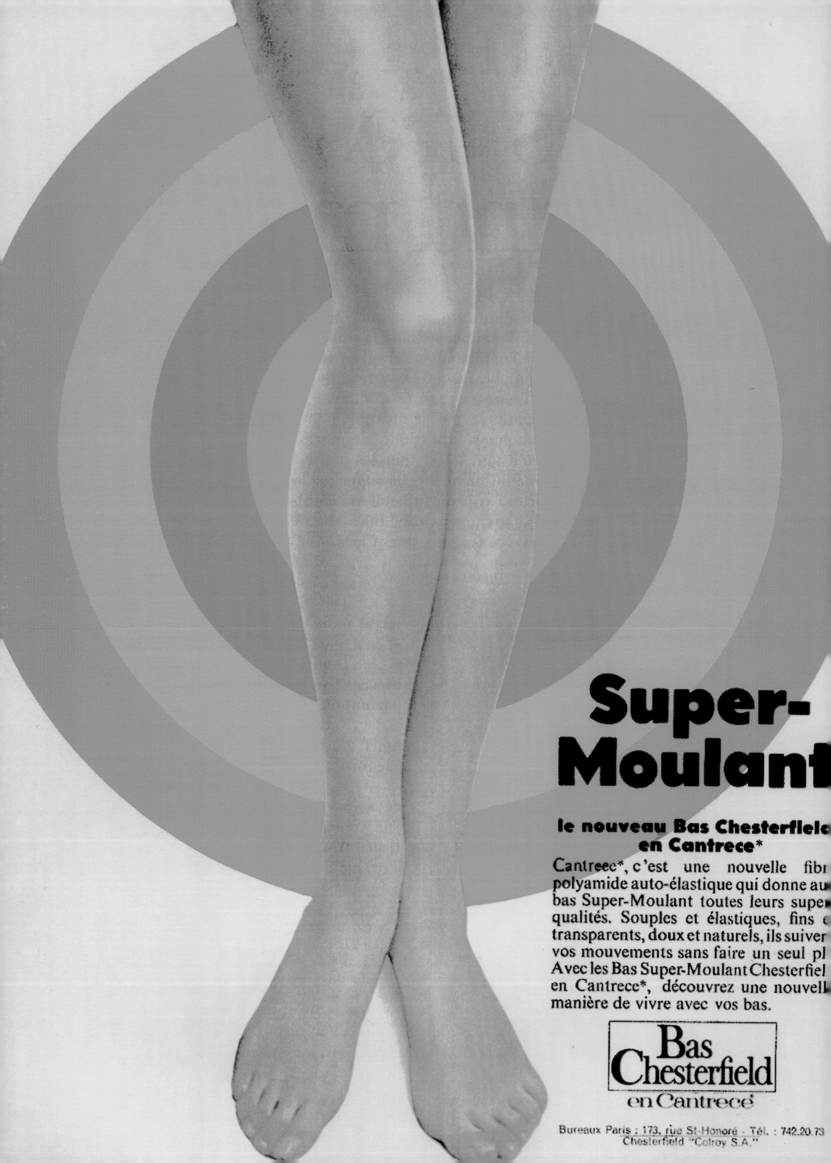

Super-Moulant

**le nouveau Bas Chesterfield
en Cantrece***

Cantreec*, c'est une nouvelle fibr
polyamide auto-élastique qui donne au
bas Super-Moulant toutes leurs super
qualités. Souples et élastiques, fins e
transparents, doux et naturels, ils suiver
vos mouvements sans faire un seul pl
Avec les Bas Super-Moulant Chesterfiel
en Cantrece*, découvrez une nouvell
manière de vivre avec vos bas.

**Bas
Chesterfield**
en Cantrecé

Bureaux Paris : 173, rue St-Honoré · Tél. : 742.20.73
Chesterfield "Colroy S.A."

bas taillunic

création Chesterfield

voile super-extensible

15 deniers
1er choix
fibre polyamide

le 1er bas
qui se met
à vos
mesures

GMP / BREVET INTERNATIONAL - FRANCE BREVET N° 1 498 043 - MODÈLE DÉPOSÉ N° 27 333

GROOVLEE
LEE-PRÈST LEESURES'
In a wide choice of styles, fabrics and colors, starting at $8.

Announcing today's go-anywhere, do-anything Hush Puppies.

That's right. Go anywhere. To a football game. A party. The office. Wherever you go, these new Hush Puppies will get you there looking just great. Comfort's still the key, of course. Always has been with Hush Puppies. But these new shoes—they've got style. Lots of it. From loafers to ties. Boots to golf shoes. In Breathin' Brushed Pigskin® or smooth leather. And the colors—they're right out of fall's family album. Browns. Greens. Rusty tans. See them today. The new go-anywhere, do-anything Hush Puppies. You'll like 'em. Prices go about $11 to $18.

Hush Puppies

AMERICAN STYLE...   POINTES BOUTONNEES !

SALUT !...   CAMBRIDGE OF CALIFORNIA

COLORIS ET DESSINS NOUVEAUX - MATIÈRES NOBLES ET RUSTIQUES
CHEMISE AMÉRICAINE

CAMBRIDGE
* OF *
CALIFORNIA

the shirts on RSG! or appear in the weekly music papers. Mods began making these sort of shirts themselves by either sewing on initials or patterns (Roger Daltrey made up some for The Who). Eventually a sharp-eyed clothing company began importing sweat shirts from US colleges such as Yale University or Harvard or from state souvenir stores. This sharp turnaround from the suits was more to do with money than sense of style. As the movement attracted more and more younger kids to it, this sort of clothing was more in their price bracket.

The hardcore Mods and faces hated the casual approach and stepped up their tailor-made apparel, claiming that the less sophisticated styles were watering down the whole emphasis of what Mod was about. This was a futile argument, albeit a correct one, for as the movement gathered momentum, so more and more people were attracted to it. They in turn brought new ideas, which broadened the scene and, by implication, led it closer and closer to the mainstream.

HATS for MODS
FABULOUS FOR STYLE, QUALITY, COMFORT & VALUE
69/6

Send now for this hat, the very latest offer from Modique. High Crown, high ribbon & ½" braided brim puts you way out ahead. This is a hand finished product with leather interior band, smart lining, and is fully waterproofed. Don't miss this offer! Avoid disappointment! Use the coupon below to ORDER NOW!!
COLOURS: *MIDNIGHT BLUE, DONKEY BROWN, SLATE GREY*

SEND **69/6** TO: MODIQUE · 44 STATION LANE HORNCHURCH · ESSEX

STATE COLOUR | Name.................................
Address.................................

SIZE ....

NME 21/2 | BLOCK LETTERS PLEASE

As more and more younger kids came in to Mod, a gang element began to emerge. Many people, including historians, assume that Mods had only one natural enemy, the Rockers! The fact was they tended to fight with one another more than anyone else until, that is, the media caught up with events and seized on one incident, the notorious seaside battle of 1964.

MOD

EYE VIEW
SCENE
THE
GREAT
MOVEMENT

I HATE BEATLES

AUGUST

THE MOD

1/6

THE WINTER'S
TALE IS PLASTIC

□ □ □

THE MAN IS
MADE OF LEATHER

□ □ □

HERE AND THERE
WITH JILL DE JEY

□ □ □

THE LATEST
MOD MODES

MOD

THE CRISP MAG
FOR WITH ITS
FESTIVE FASHIONS FOR
MODS
THE MOD SCENE
by VICKI WICKHAM

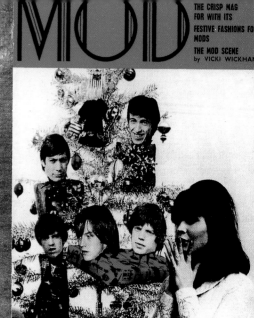

THE MOD

THE MAG FOR
THE
SWITCHED ON MOD
VICKI WICKHAM
says . . .
NEW STYLES FOR
THE NEW YEAR

1/6

JANUARY 1965

1 2
8 9   14
1
22 23   28
29 30

JEAN

THE MOD

VICKI
THE MOD   JULY
PUZZLE?

THE mod

MOD MODES FOR SUMMER
LATEST MALE MOD GEAR
ANGELA'S PASSION FLOWERS

JUNE
1/6

THE MOD'S

1/6

AUGUST

MONTHLY

THE MOD'S

1/6

APRIL

MONTHLY

FASHIONS
for the
FUTURE

TWO-PAGE
EXCLUSIVE by
CATHY
McGOWAN

SHOES · HATS
COATS
RECORDS
DANCES

MODS IN
YOUR AREA

THE MOD'S

1/6

JULY

MONTHLY

the MOD

BIBA'S MAGICAL TRANSFORMATION SCENE
AUTUMN LEAVES
THE LINGERIE LARK
......
SEPTEMBER 1/6

WHERE have all the Mods gone? It was not so long ago that the latest thing were Mods. They were the people who appeared as the dancers at "Ready Steady Go": Cathy McGowan said she was a Mod. The national dailies called her Mother Mod McGowan. They held a great Mod Ball. Mods were also something that fought with Rockers at the seaside. Mods rode scooters. Mods wore their skirts long when everybody else wore their's short. Mods had razor-cut hairdos, wore anoraks and lettered T-shirts. Mods were thin and wary eyed. So wrote one newspaper. Mods did strange dances . . . now, suddenly all the Mods have gone—the Rockers still seem to be about . . . have they won one last great battle and exterminated all the Mods?

Continued on page 2

THE MODS

HOW DARE YOU?
VICKI WICKHAM says
THE FASHION MAG FOR MODS
FEB 1/6
PARTY UNMENTION-ABLES
MAKE UP TO TOMORROW

DS MONTHLY — THE MOD SCENE

B.B.C. T.V.2's BEAT ROOM

are you a real MOD?

its CRISP
its Crunchy
SEPT.

Down Carnaby Street

THE MOD'S

HERBALS
1/6
MOD MAKE UP

Mod Style for Autumn
HAIR STYLE OFFER!!

THE MO

The Mod

KEEP ... TRENDS · THE BAREFOOT GIRLS
MIDNIGHT MOD FASHION SHOW
MAY 1/6

THE MOD

THE CRISP MAG FOR WITH ITS VICKI WICKHAM SAYS . . . MOD FASHIONS FOR THE 5th ETC. ETC.

NOVEMBER 1/6

THE MOD

1/6
OCTOBER

Mad Mods * The Rolling Stones * Vicki Wickhams page * A Mod Winter * All the Top Fashions * The Crisp Crunchy With it Mag For Crisp With its etc.

THE MOD'S

1/6
MARCH
MONTHLY

SHOES
HATS
COATS
RECORDS
DANCES
LATEST "DOLLYROCKER" DRESSES
AB MOD GEAR OF OP MODS

THE MOD'S

1/6
MAY
MONTHLY

EXCLUSIVE ARTICLES BY CATHY McGOWAN and VICKI WICKHAM

SHOES · HATS
COATS
RECORDS
DANCES
MODS IN YOUR AREA

THE MOD'S

1/6
JUNE
MONTHLY

EXCLUSIVE ARTICLES BY CATHY McGOWAN and VICKI WICKHAM

THE ONLY MOD MAGAZINE WITH EXCLUSIVE MOD FASHIONS

thought Rockers were all greasy old leather-clad Teddy boys and Rockers thought Mods were little nancy boy effeminate queers. In fact, the two factions had lived together quite peacefully until the punch-ups gained national attention. There was even one London dance hall, Leyton Baths, that had a white line painted along one side of the dance floor that was intended to segregate the Mods and Rockers when they danced. Not ideal, but apparently it actually worked for a while.

Graham Hughes: *"I remember going to the Hammersmith Odeon to see Chuck Berry and there was all the Mods down the front and next to the Mods would be Teds and Rockers. There's this whole myth that Mods only liked one sort of music, 'Soul', but that wasn't the case. Rock and Roll wasn't just a Teds or a Rockers thing. Mods went to see all sorts of people, Lord Sutch even, and bought their records. The first record I bought was 'Singing The Blues' by Diane Mitchell and Tommy Steele did a cover of it. Obviously Diane Mitchell's was the better one and it's true we didn't like covers and we would listen to American R&B. A couple of people got away with it but I can't think of many, we wanted originals. I suppose Alexis Korner got away with it, Cyril Davies and Burt Weedon. Burt Weedon was the guy that taught everyone to play the guitar, everyone in this country heard him first."*

Richard Barnes: *"I put in my Who book for a joke that Pete Townshend learnt his Burt Weedon chords and it's become legend now and people write to him from all over the world and ask 'What did you learn from Burt Weedon?'"*

Ken Browne: *"There had always been Rockers at places like the Lyceum on a lunch-time or at gigs but there wasn't any trouble. The trouble was always with the Mods fighting other Mods but after '64 it was Mods and Rockers. We did hate Rockers. All my mates were working-class Mods, so it's not a class thing because the Rockers were predominantly working class also. We just hated their filthy, dirty, scruffy, smelly, leather jackets and grease and dirt and studs, what a fucking*

Mods, rockers and knockers

It used to be the Young Ones . . . then it was the Wild Ones. Now it's Mods and Rockers. What these louts do — the layabout louts who cause trouble — has little to do with Melody Maker. Except that we deplore violence like any other reasonable body.

But when people start trying to drag Beat music into this lunacy, the red mist comes down over our eyes.

A few young idiots use violence in seaside towns and the next thing you know, Beat stars are being asked to comment on the riots.

Why? Why not ask teenage butchers? Or teenage grocers? Or teenage rat-catchers?

Before you know it, the young rioters will be called Beat fans.

Or even jazz fans — heaven knows, they've been going through it for years.

Lay off young people's music. Like long hair, it's harmless until the knockers get to work.

THE EDITOR

The Bank

He is one of forty-four boys interviewed. His mother is dead. Part of his home has been destroyed by fire. He has seven brothers, five sisters. It is a close-knit family, but there is no room in the home for amusement.

Away from home's dreariness, in his bright Mod clothes, the boy finds a gayer life at places like Margate.

A REPORT OF GREAT POINT THIS SUNDAY: 44 MODS AND ROCKERS CONVICTED AFTER WHITSUN'S RIOTS EXPLAIN THEIR MOTIVES..

USING his magistrate's freedom, Dr. Simpson called them petty sawdust Caesars when they came up in his Margate court last Whit Monday. With another Bank Holiday weekend upon us, it is the right moment to check to see how many of the cliches about Mods and Rockers have any truth in them.

We have carried out a questionnaire survey of the forty-four young men and teenagers who came up at Margate on Whit Monday. All of them were found guilty and given sentences that varied from three months' jail to a conditional discharge.

by Paul Barker

WITH DR ALAN LITTLE

One thing that emerges is how lightly the group most likely to be influenced — the defendants' friends — took the sentences. It raises the whole question of what did Margate stop?

Altogether the teenagers were very ready to talk, but their parents were less keen till they were sure it meant no further personal publicity.

The big reason given for both reactions was the feeling that the sentences were unfair.

Four people felt they'd been mistaken for a typical Mod or Rocker. Only six admitted they had been in any fighting. Twenty claimed mostly to have been doing nothing or else moving away from trouble when they were arrested.

GAMES

ONE boy, still at a grammar school, told me that he and some other Mods had been playing "childish games" among themselves on the beach.

There was no violence to this, he maintained, though he admitted that earlier some Rockers had been hit over the head with broken deck-chairs. He had "not been doing the hitting."

As he was coming off the beach with a piece of wood in his hand that he had been kicking around on the sands, he tossed it on to a pile of rubbish by the steps.

A policeman said: "Pick that up, laddie," the boy told me. "Like a fool, I did. He arrested me, and I was charged with carrying an offensive weapon."

He could see that, faced with an apparent riot, the police needed to arrest somebody.

But he didn't think he should have been up on this charge.

He pleaded guilty in court because he felt it would be best to get it over with, and was fined £75 for this and threatening behaviour (his first offences).

For all except ten of our sample, it was a first offence that brought them to court in Margate.

The average age of defendants was about eighteen, so these were not habitual delinquents.

Twenty-two said they would make sure they weren't mixed up in anything like this again. Most gave their Margate punishment as the reason, or fear of worse next time.

"The fine is fifty good reasons for not doing it again," said a Mod who had had to find most of the money from his savings for clothes.

But several cited their night in the cells as the worst part of the punishment: "I had to sleep on a stone floor, and I was only given two pieces of toast and a cup of tea in twenty-five hours."

There were still some who thought "It's a free country, I'll go to the trouble again, if I want." One Mod has already been in a dispute with Rockers at Brighton since Whitsun.

JOKE

WHATEVER the recipients themselves thought of their punishment, their friends thought it "a great joke," or "they looked up to me after that."

One 21-year-old was given "a Beatle reception" by his mates when he came back from prison.

At worst friends thought the mistake had been to be caught. Only the grammar school boy faced a split reaction. "My Mod friends thought it was great. My school friends said I was an idiot."

Some were genuinely at the Margate outbreak by accident. One lived there: five said they visited the resort regularly.

A Midlands hosiery worker had booked a flat there with some friends three months before. He claimed not to know the difference between a Mod and a Rocker.

He was arrested, he said, when "walking down the sands," which is "what you're there to do."

Prudently, he is spending August Bank Holiday at Butlin's, Bognor Regis.

Only one person went to Margate alone. Everyone else went with at least one friend, or the intention of meeting up with friends there.

The groupiness of Margate only reflected the way a normal week was spent. One Rocker who lived in digs was the only person to mention solo activity.

"I've more time to think than most Rockers. As soon as they get home, there's a family screaming: 'Where have you been till this time?'"

But he wasn't fond of his solitude. "Oh, yes, sure I'll marry. This is what'll drive me to it," waving a hand at the small room with its unmade bed.

Of those who classed themselves as Mods or Rockers, the pattern of week-day evenings was fairly similar.

They would be out every night but one — probably Wednesday, when cash was low.

That night they would spend with the family; others were spent with friends, mostly the same group, usually all male.

Girl-friends are compartmented off from the main part of life. One boy takes his girl dancing at a rhythm and blues club, takes her home, then goes out with his mates.

On Saturday, it is work or home in the morning; shopping for Mods or a caff for Rockers in the afternoon; dancing in the evening. Home again for Sunday morning and afternoon, and a dance again at night.

Rockers are more likely to slip an old-fashioned visit to the pictures in somewhere. Neither group watches television much. Mods listen to the radio rather more often.

Fourteen of those interviewed classed themselves as Mods (counting in the punctilious Peckham teenager who said it was all Stylists now: this subtlety hadn't yet reached suburbanites and provincials); nine were Rockers; and twelve said they were neither.

A few of the mid-group aligned with Rockers, and one or two were outside the rivalry altogether. But to an interviewer's eye, the rest looked like Mods.

STAID

THE Mods were generally more staid. With an average age of 19, they were a year nearer the oldies than the Mods and Rockers proper. They spent more time during the week with their families — while Mods and Rockers were out with the group.

When they went out, Mods were slightly more likely to be at dance clubs than Rockers.

("Whenever I go to a dance hall it's all Mod," a Rocker mourned. "And as soon as I've learnt the twist and the shake they're off on to something else that I can't do. I can only dance at parties.")

But the main difference between the rivals was that one group spent its time being Mod, the other being Rocker.

The Mods and Rockers had a positive and negative image of themselves: the positive revealed by how they saw themselves, the negative by how they saw their rivals. Both saw themselves mainly in terms of dress: either the

Holiday Offenders

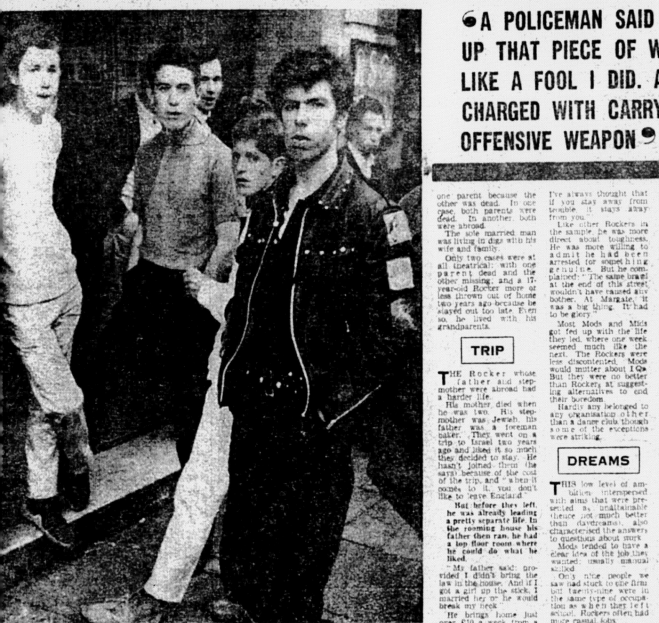

The Mod boy from the family of thirteen mingles with other Mods (and a passing Rocker) as he goes into a seaside disc club.

6A POLICEMAN SAID "PICK UP THAT PIECE OF WOOD." LIKE A FOOL I DID. AND WAS CHARGED WITH CARRYING AN OFFENSIVE WEAPON9
—a grammar school Mod.

one parent because the other was dead. In one case, both parents were dead. In another, both were abroad.

The sole married man was living in digs with his wife and family.

Only two cases were at all theatrical: with one parent dead and the other missing; and a 17-year-old Rocker more or less thrown out of home two years ago because he stayed out too late. Even so, he lived with his grandparents.

TRIP

THE Rocker whose father and stepmother were abroad had a harder life.

His mother died when he was two. His stepmother was Jewish, his father was a foreman baker. They went on a trip to Israel two years ago and liked it so much they decided to stay. He hasn't joined them (he says) because of the cost of the trip, and "when it comes to it, you don't like to leave England."

But before they left, he was already leading a pretty separate life. In the rooming house his father then ran, he had a top floor room where he could do what he liked.

"My father said: provided I didn't bring the law in the house. And if I got a girl up the stick, I married her or he would break my neck."

He brings home just over £10 a week from a semi-skilled building job. He pays £3 a week for a single room. It cost him £1 a week to run his Thunderbird bike till he sold it because of the Margate fine.

His room was hung with trophies: cowboy hats and spurs; drawing of James Dean, with dates of birth and death; buffalo horns fixed to bed head.

RESPECT

HIS attitudes were pleasantly traditional. He respected his "guvnor" at work. "If there's anyone I'd like to grow up like, it's my Dad."

"Last year, I had my own gang. There were about 100 of us. We all went down to Margate then and had a great time in the arcades. We didn't hit any old ladies or smash any shop windows.

"This time he knew there was trouble in the wind. "But I didn't think it would affect us.

I've always thought that if you stay away from trouble, it stays away from you."

Like other Rockers in the sample, he was more direct about toughness. He was more willing to admit he had been arrested for something genuine. But he complained: "The same brawl at the end of this street wouldn't have caused any bother. At Margate, it was a big thing. It had to be glory."

Most Mods and Mids got fed up with the life they led, where one week seemed much like the next. The Rockers were less discontented. Mods would mutter about I.Q. But they were no better than Rockers at suggesting alternatives to end their boredom.

Hardly any belonged to any organisation other than a dance club, though some of the exceptions were striking.

DREAMS

THIS low level of ambition, interspersed with aims that were presented as unattainable (hence not much better than daydreams), also characterised the answers to questions about work.

Mods tended to have a clear idea of the job they wanted; usually manual skilled.

Only nine people we saw had stuck to one firm, but twenty-nine were in the same type of occupation as when they left school. Rockers often had more casual jobs.

To the wide question "What would you like to do for the rest of your life?" the answers were revealing. Twelve wanted their present job; nine a slightly higher position; and eleven a violent change.

A meat porter wanted to be a Mayfair drinking club owner; a cook an airline pilot.

Why these gaps between dream and reality? The replies became vague and implausible: "You need friends" to become a lorry driver.

It would be some immovable obstacle like that: lack of money, perhaps or fate.

The dustman who got a Beatle reception after jail wanted to be "something useful which will do good as a probation officer." He

expected to stay a dustman, however.

If friends thought the convictions a joke, and employers didn't know or were amused, parents on the other hand, were shocked and angry.

The mother was generally more upset than the father. In the case of the grammar schoolboy, his parents were worried about his future career and kept the name out of the local paper.

For most other parents, after all, it was also their child's first appearance in court. By now they have mostly settled down to bitterness at the fine and the charge.

Where the boys could not afford the fine or weren't given time to pay, the parents were the main people who paid up or helped to pay.

One boy's parents are paying him back half the fine, though he has paid it into court himself: they think it so unfair.

That is a bizarre exception, but it cast some light on the relation between these parents and their young. (The young are even sometimes exemplary; three-quarters of the Mods give over a third of their take-home pay to their parents, one gives half. Rockers give from a fifth to a quarter.)

WORRIES

ROCKERS in their self-sufficient way, hardly ever tell their parents about their worries. Their parents usually want to know what they're doing, but rarely find out.

They have bursts of complaining about their sons' behaviour. Their sons are under no illusion that they behave as their parents would like it, but they don't mind.

Mods usually tell parents about their worries, and they quite often tell what they are doing if they are asked. Parents rarely complain about their behaviour, though the Mods feel they only occasionally behave as their parents would like. But also they only occasionally care.

It is surprising when so many lived at home, that so few parents had any clue they were going to Margate last Whitsun.

---

known smooth getup of the Mods or the leather jacket and faded jeans of the Rockers.

The negative images are different. Rockers see Mods as effeminate. They can wear skirts if they like, so long as I don't pick one up as a girl." That was a tolerant opinion.

Mods see Rockers as evenly and dirty: "Long, greasy hair—they use axle grease. They stink of petrol fumes."

Neither group particularly defines itself by its attitudes, though one Mod said: "Mods can talk about themselves. Rockers just say: 'Huh, have a cuppa tea'; that's it." (To which the comeback: "Rockers have a healthier attitude to life. You won't find any drugs and not much drinking.")

The Rocker outlook

(for this boy) seemed to come down to straightforwardness and an overriding interest: "A Rocker has his motor-bike. You'll find him talking or generally playing the fool, but mostly he dreams, eats and sleeps motor-bikes."

'POOR'

THE reported invasion of Margate by scooters and motor-bikes is exaggerated. Of our sample only seven went by bike or scooter.

Thirteen used public transport, twelve went by car, and one hitched. The Rockers made more use of public transport than Mods.

"Rockers are poorer than Mods," one Rocker said. This was scarcely true. The average take-home pay of the whole

sample was £11 per week, for Rockers £10.

In our size of sample, it wasn't a significant difference. But it was significant that Mids took home £13 10s.

And it was true that Mods came from a rather better-off background and could look forward to steadier future earnings.

"Mods are more likely to be learning a trade" was a more accurate statement.

The typical Rocker had an unskilled manual job; the typical Mod was a semi-skilled manual worker.

The Rocker's father was a semi-skilled worker; the Mod's was non-manual.

The boys themselves did not remark on any distinction between them in terms of class, and the lines weren't rigidly drawn.

Five Mods were unskilled. No Rocker had

a non-manual or skilled manual job.

People joined the one group or the other, they said, because they liked that style of dressing, or because they despised the other style.

Two Mods said they spent £25 the previous month; four Rockers had spent hardly anything.

No Rocker claimed to have spent more than £12; no Mod less than £4.

Mods, Rockers and Mids were all likely to have a record player, and somewhat less likely to have a transistor set.

No one was heavily tied up with hire purchase. The trappings of affluence had usually either been bought cash down or given as presents.

We must shoot down the broken-home cliche as well. Only eight in the sample were not living with both parents.

One son was living with

This survey, commissioned by the magazine New Society, was also sponsored by Granada TV—with the co-operation of Dr. Alan Little of the London School of Economics.

nightmare. We used to run the gauntlet. Every time we went to The Starlight after that it was bad news. There was a council estate where I lived and we had to go through it every night to get home and you would have to run the gauntlet of about 20 Rockers that were in their early twenties and we were only about 15 or 16 years old. We had to get through that lot and there was nearly always a fight and we never had a chance but when we got older the roles seemed to reverse a bit. Some Rockers actually became Mods. They changed over, some of the guys on the council estate definitely changed. There was a bloke called Bob Strutton for one, he went from being a Rocker to a Mod and he turned out to be a really top Mod. His clothes, his scooter were unbelievable but that didn't happen very often.

"The worst time I remember was in Enfield. I had this bloody bright multi-coloured striped blazer and red shoes on, my hair all bouffanted up and I was with my mate John Hall, who had lent his leather jacket to some bird down there. We had to go and get it back. We had to go on a train because the scooters were totally unreliable to go as far as Enfield. We went to this youth club that she told us to meet her at. It was some sort of church hall thing and it was empty. She was right down the front and there were about five or six Mod girls there. We walked up to them looking totally outrageous. John even had eye make-up on because that was the stage of all that going on. We were talking to these Mod girls and the place filled, literally filled up with Rockers. About a hundred of them walked in almost in one hit and there was just us two down the front. I was absolutely shitting myself. I thought 'How are we going to get out of here. I couldn't see a side door or side exit, so we had to walk through all these guys, the whole lot of them and they all parted. It was all 'Hello Darling' and tripping you up and the rest of it. I thought we'd made it because we got as far as the door, John was much smaller that me so they didn't pick on him but they decided I would do and I got absolutely hammered. I got slung out face forward by four of them. They got hold of my arms and legs and slung me out on the gravel, face first in the gravel. The girls had totally and utterly stitched us up but we got the coat back, a full-length blue leather."

Richard Barnes: "The press reports changed so much every one was seen as violent thugs and not many of them actually were. I remember word going around the club I was running that there was going to be this big fight down in Clacton. No, no that was it, there wasn't a mention of a fight, a lot of Mods were going to Clacton anyway because just like now, people went to the coast on bank holidays. Mods didn't invent going to the coast. Clacton was tiny with nothing to do, so a lot of kids just started pulling pranks, nicking the odd stuff here and there and generally making a nuisance of themselves in the arcade, or what have you. When the police finally came, everyone ran along the beach and I think some old lady got knocked over and it was called a riot on TV that night, it was ridiculous."

Dicky Dodson: "That riot at Clacton wasn't really a riot, not between Mods and Rockers anyway. You'd get about 40 Mods and four Rockers and all the Mods would run for it. Except for a few tough guys but there were never enough Rockers at Clacton, Brighton or anywhere. It was always maybe two dozen Rockers and 400 Mods."

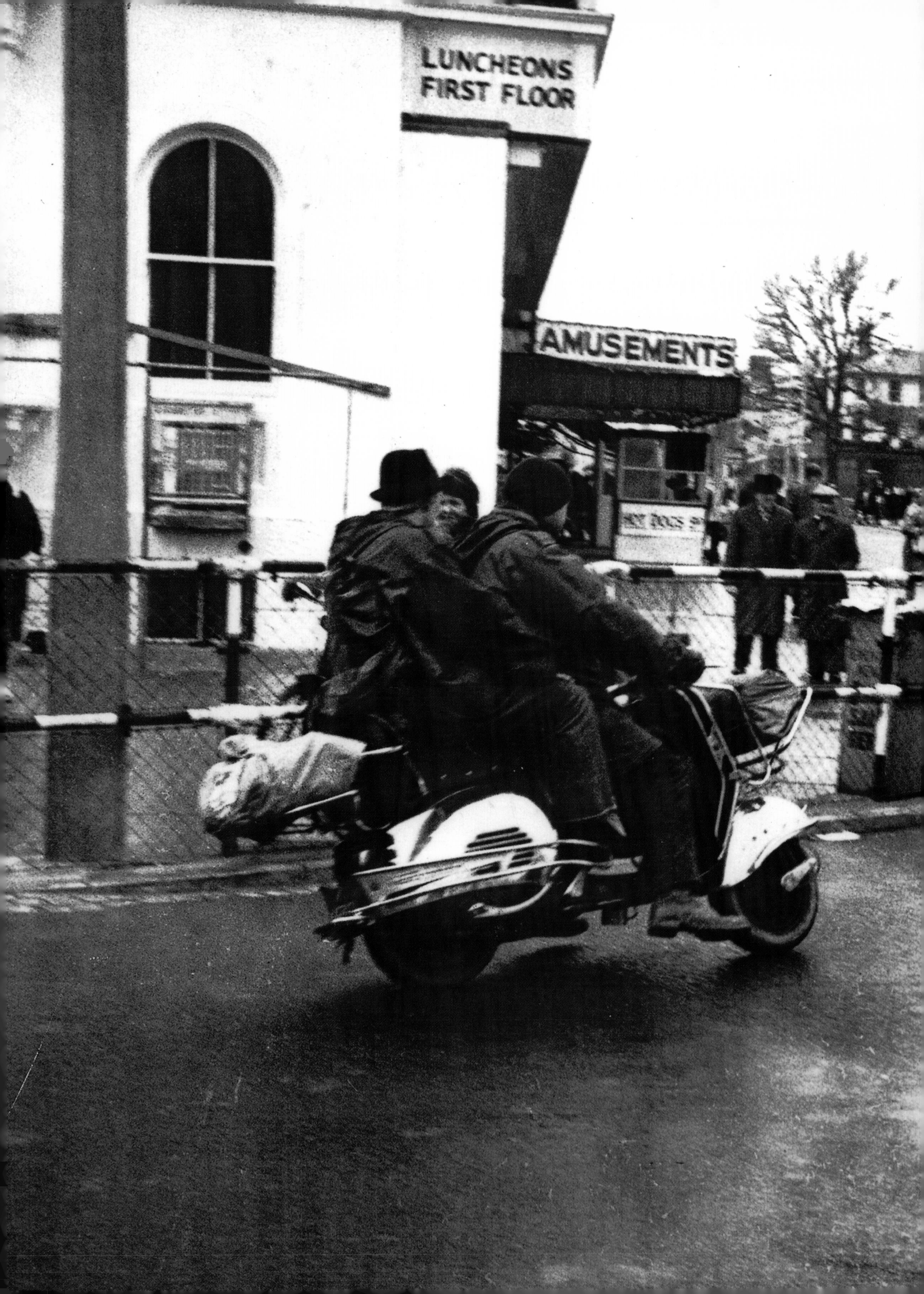
LUNCHEONS
FIRST FLOOR
AMUSEMENTS
HOT DOGS

This wasn't how the evening news reported the skirmishes — they described the trouble that day as an all-out youth war. And the result of all the press coverage couldn't have been more predictable. The news of a siege of Mods at Clacton resulted in hundreds more Mods descending on the tiny resort. Followed closely by hordes of Fleet Street journalists and cameramen intent on getting a story and picture from the front.

Dicky Dodson: *"Those sort of Mods that went looking for trouble on the second day of the bank holiday weekend were the beginning of the skinheads, really. It was the Fred Perry brigade, not what I knew to be Mods, and of course there was nothing for them to do there because all the shops and cafés were shut.*

"The press wanted a story and almost willed them to start trouble and that time they did, but it wasn't much to do with Mods and Rockers. There were a couple of Rockers but it was mostly Mods fighting the police and annoying shopkeepers."

The tabloids were delighted anyway and featured the riots on the front of every paper with banner headlines such as 'Wild Ones Invade Seaside — 97 Arrests' and 'Scooter Gangs Beat Up Clacton'. From now on, the Mods would be forever linked to violence and rampage.

Johnny Moke: *"From then on, 1964/1965, it wasn't Modernism anymore, it was something different. Attitudes changed within and without, it wasn't being modern. It was more towards being a member of a gang and that's not what we were all about. We were about style, fashion and lifestyle and the next thing, it's all focused on Clacton or Brighton beach and there were thousands of kids and they were all losing their things on the beach and trying to find them. We weren't part of it anymore, we looked at them and they looked at us and we were completely different. They were just a tribe, they weren't setting themselves apart. We were always striving and setting ourselves apart, trying to move one step ahead or forward. You were never with the gang."*

From now on, the Mods would be for

By MIRROR REPORTER

ON the run they went yesterday— the Mods and Rockers.

A lot of them had ridden into Hastings on their motor scooters and motor bikes on Saturday.

But yesterday many of them were on foot.

And — as these two pictures show — everywhere they went, on the beach or through the town, they were running . . . running . . . running . . .

They ran in the STREETS of this usually quiet seaside town with its old hotels . . .

When one of them ran, they all ran. When one of them clapped, they all clapped. When one of them jeered, they all jeered.

The turbulent teenaged tide seemed sometimes in danger of flooding the normally sedate seaside town. Then the emotional current would change—and sweep on to the BEACH.

There, the crash of scores of feet trampling the shingle drowned the gentle lapping of the tide. And there, at one stage, dozens of youngsters fled before a lone policeman.

ANXIOUS

Crowds milled around aimlessly. Shopkeepers looked on anxiously as the mob swept by.

Hard - pressed police drove round in circles trying to keep up as the Mods changed direction every few minutes, always running , . .

But why? No one knows — not even the runners.

ON T

ONE policema

DAY. The place, HASTINGS. The tempo, QUICK, very QUICK

E RUN

The Mods and Rockers invade . . but this time it's an 'itchy feet' invasion

nked to violence and rampage.

MANY Mods scurrying across the pebbly beach at Hastings yesterday

Daily Mail
News Chronicle

NO. 21,234   FOR QUEEN AND COMMONWEALTH

AS POLICE SEND MODS
AND ROCKERS PACKING . . .

Mystery on the beach

Comment
If it hadn't happened

EVERYONE knows that an older world perished 50 years ago today—August 4, 1914—when the Great War began.

The second world war gave new impetus to the movements which had started 25 years before. It was, in fact, a renewal of the conflict.

But what would the world have been like if this war —or these wars—had not happened? It is a fascinating field for speculation.

Nothing remained unaltered after history's most terrible blood-letting. The transformation was material, political, social and moral. All these aspects of life would be very different now if the guns had not gone off.

Most of the monarchies would no doubt still be in being. The class system would be more rigid than it is, though less so than it was.

There would be more pomp, snobbery and stuffiness, but we should also enjoy a stability which vanished with the European Empires.

Pressures

IN a material sense the wars, as wars always do, telescoped in a few years advances which might otherwise have taken a century.

In 1914 the aeroplane was a kite, a stringbag. By 1919 it was a vehicle of international transport. In 1939 it was a 300 m.p.h. "prop." By 1945 it had become a 600 m.p.h. jet.

Had it not been for the pressures of war we might still be hailing transatlantic flight as the wonder of the age. We should certainly be nowhere near the conquest of space or the era of nuclear power.

We could mention motor-cars, communications, radio, electronics, plastics, artificial fibres, new foods. The list is endless. All were either invented for war or developed at a pace impossible without it.

Barriers

THESE things have had a profound effect on class distinctions. Even without them the wars would have broken these barriers down. With them, the process is speedier.

Old conventions have disappeared and ideas of morality have assumed new forms. Such "movements" were already in motion during the Nineties of last century and the early years of this one.

But it was one short post-war decade, the Twenties, which gave impetus and authority to the new freedoms. It set the tone and 1939-1945 confirmed it.

The Great War raised the condition of the people, though this was masked by the Depression. The second war led to undreamed-of standards of living.

Casualties

LIFE as we know it today would almost certainly never come about even if there had been no wars, though not in the way, perhaps for 2064.

There would have been evolution instead, and not the all-embracing revolution which has produced our noisy, mobile, exciting, but frenzied age.

Owing to the fearful need to fight and survive, we have been rushed into a strange new world without having time to adjust to it.

This is what the wars have done. The dead, civilian and military, numbered at least 60,000,000. The question is whether what we enjoy, or endure, today was worth that awful price.

The answer must be an unqualified: "No!" Fifty million times: "No!"

By
CHRISTOPHER UNDERWOOD

MODS and Rockers were asked last night to help solve a death mystery of the 1964 Battle of Hastings.

Police asked youths involved in the disturbances:

Who was the penniless boy Mod washed ashore at dawn yesterday with nothing in his pockets to reveal his identity?

Do you know how he died? Is any member of a Mod group missing?

A postmortem is believed to have established that death was due to drowning. But the mystery of how the boy got in the water remained.

Mr. Donald Brown, Chief Constable of Hastings, said late last night that no progress had been made in identifying the victim.

"I have an open mind regarding this death, but at the moment there is no evidence to suggest crime," he said.

The Mod who died was aged only 15-17. He had a dimpled chin, mid-brown wavy hair and was 5ft. 2in.

He wore jeans, a white pullover and a blue blazer.

He was found at 4.55 a.m. by teenagers who had been sleeping on the beach. One of them, 18-year-old Leslie Barnes, of South Ockendon, Essex, said:

"When I woke up I saw something floating in the water. At first I thought it was a dummy. But as I helped others pull him out of the water I realised he was a youth."

Bruises

"He seemed to have been dead for several hours."

Seventeen-year-old Brian Lawrence, of Staines, said: "When we pulled him out I saw what looked like bruises on his back and face."

Inside the boy's blazer was a tag bearing the name of Brent and Collins Man's Shop, at 69 Alexandra Road, Romford, Southend, Barking and Brentwood, Essex.

Underneath his blue jeans the boy wore a pair of Hungarian-made blue football shorts and yellow bathing trunks.

Hustled out of Hastings

By Daily Mail Reporter

POLICE at Hastings began to disperse early today after complete victory over the Mods and Rockers.

A spokesman said : "The town is very quiet. The trouble seems to be over."

Police still guarded the almost deserted promenade. But most of the invaders had been dispirited and beaten.

Seperated

How was it done? Hastings Chief Constable Mr. Donald Brown said: "It was a matter of reinforcements and professionalism."

Local police, reinforced by men from neighbouring forces and the "flying" squad from London, separated the Mods and Rockers to opposite ends of the sea front.

Then the police got the Mods on the move and hustled them out of town.

For two days the gangs

were broken up and kept on the move. And the public and the local tradesmen warmly praised the police tactics.

Seventy-four people were arrested during the two days of trouble. Among them were nine at midnight—and some 50 youths appeared again in court this morning.

More than 100 Mods from Hastings swarmed off a train at Charing Cross late last night. A few minutes later police found 5,000 in the train refreshment rooms and handbar ripped off.

Police at Margate arrested 51 youths who were fighting broken out on the beaches.

For 24 minutes scores of police using snorts of opposing sides along the sea-front.

Trouble also came to Great Yarmouth, as scuffles between youths and police went on.

61

AND MINISTER CALLS ROAD TOLL DEPRESSING

By Daily Mail Reporter

SEVENTEEN road deaths on Sunday brought the provisional total for the first three days of the holiday to 61—compared with 50 last year.

Sunday's total was three more than in 1963.

Lord Chesham, Parliamentary Secretary to the Transport Ministry, said last night it is a pretty depressing because there is no obvious explanation why the figures are up.

Perhaps the carefree holiday mood is one factor.

"Most people try to drive responsibly but the impatient, selfish and inconsiderate minority is too high."

Lord Chesham said that Ministers would like to know whether high-speed driving or holidaymakers contributed to the road toll.

The holiday heatwave brought a late rush home last night—with about 250,000 cars joining the main roads.

London had not had a warmer August Bank Holiday since 1926, though the maximum of 79 degrees at Kew only equalled the levels of 1946, 1955 and 1957. The 1938 peak was 84.

Elsewhere in the South-East the maximum was 80 degrees, the warmest Bank Holiday Monday for seven years. The temperature reached 82 at Thorney Island and Southampton.

In London, crowds flocked to the parks. The temperature rose five degrees in two hours after noon.

There were 250,000 people at Hampstead Heath, and a record 30,000 at Woburn Abbey, home of the Duke of Bedford.

ROLL U

In this, as in so many other aspects of youth culture, the British were light years behind the Continentals, the Italians in particular — but Mods couldn't afford a plane ticket to Rome or Milan just to get their hair cut.

The next bank holiday was Whitsun weekend and Clacton went on 24-hour alert. It needn't have bothered, though. Nobody went there! It seemed that everybody had already tried Clacton and declared it shut. This time the main flashpoints were widespread and took in Margate, Bournemouth, Brighton and even inner London itself.

The press were helpfully on hand once again, cameras and notebooks at the ready to report back from the front line of the latest youth invasion. Record numbers of arrests and violent disturbances were declared as actual punch-ups between the rival factions were captured on film for the first time. The inordinate amounts of press coverage once again outrageously exaggerated the extent of the troubles but this time there was undeniable proof of violence on film. These youngsters were apparently no more than demented, pilled-up yobbos and the papers felt vindicated enough to say so. Vitriolic speeches by outraged law-abiding citizens, judges and police chiefs filled the dailies, beneath headlines that painted the perpetrators of violence as 'Vermin', 'Mentally Unstable' and 'Petty Little Sawdust Caesars'.

'Mods and Rockers' became the new media catch-phrase, a single mouthful linked together for all time, as inseparable as Morecambe and Wise or pie and mash. In the mind of the great British public, both groups became labelled simply as vandals who habitually set out to disrupt the traditional bank holiday family day out at the seaside. All of which went a long way to alienate the older original Mods like Graham Hughes and Dicky Dodson, who viewed this newer, unruly Mod element in much the same way that the press did.

Paul Stagg: *"A prelude to football violence, skinheads, racism, you name it. They weren't Mods as we knew Mods, they were just gangs of kids dressed up. No real Mod wanted to roll about in the dirt, sand, pebbles or anything else for that matter. The clothes were still the most important factor, not fighting."*

The funniest thing was seeing the co we'll give it to them.

Unfortunately the violent image appealed to the younger Mods (pretenders or otherwise) and many of them played up to it wholeheartedly. One of the best examples of this came via an in-depth sociological probe into the lives of British youth by Charles Hambert and Jane Deverson, published in November 1964 under the title 'Generation X — Today's Generation Talking About Itself'. Hambert and Deverson interviewed John Braden, an 18-year-old Mod and a car mechanic from London just days after the Whitsun clashes. Braden had this to say: *"Yes I am a Mod and I was at Margate. I'm not ashamed of it — I wasn't the only one. I joined in a few of the fights, it was a laugh, I haven't enjoyed myself so much in a long time. It was great — the beach was like a battlefield. It was like we were taking over the country. You want to hit back at all the old geezers who try to tell us what to do. We just want to show them we're not going to take it. It was like a battlefield, I felt great, part of something important instead of just being something they look down on because you haven't passed a GCE. I know some old men were knocked down but none of them were hurt. They might've got a bit of a shock but they deserve it — they don't think about us, how we might feel.*

"It was great being in the newspapers, sure we love reading about ourselves, who doesn't? Blinkin' film stars and debs delights and social climbers hire publicity men to get their bleedin' names in the papers. We punch our way in cost free. Reading the linens afterwards is part of the kicks. Makes you feel you've done something, made people sit up and take notice. What these old squares don't realise is we've got far more guts than they ever had and don't talk to me about the bleedin' war. War is for ginks. That magistrate was protecting his own kind, you can't blame him for that but why take it out on us? They're jealous of us, that's why they make all that fuss.

"Bashin' rockers is something to do isn't it? The funniest thing was seeing the cops getting tough. If they want a fight we'll give it to them. It's something that gets to you. You don't know what it is, I can't explain it — you just go wild. There's a lot of hate in me,

Daily Mirror

3d.   Wednesday, August 5, 1964   *   No. 18,856

End of the 200-hour agony 270 ft down

MAGNIFIQUE!
ALL 9 SAVED

New Red attack on U.S. warships

From DONALD LUDLOW, Washington, Tuesday

COMMUNIST torpedo boats today attacked two American destroyers off the coast of North Vietnam.

At least two of the attacking boats were believed to have been sunk, in a three-hour battle, by the destroyers and supporting aircraft.

One of the destroyers involved was the Maddox, which was attacked by North Vietnamese torpedo boats on Sunday.

The other was the C Turner Joy, which was ordered yesterday to join the Maddox on patrol in the Gulf of Tonkin.

At least six torpedo boats took part in to-day's attack.

The two destroyers opened fire, and fighters and dive-bombers from the U.S aircraft-carriers Ticonderoga and Constellation joined in the battle.

Apart from the two ships believed sunk, two other Communist vessels were damaged.

'Kill'

There was no damage to the American ships or injury to their crews.

Yesterday—after the first attack on the Maddox—President Johnson ordered the U.S Navy to "shoot to kill" if there were any more incidents.

And as well as doubling the destroyer force off North Vietnam, he ordered the Ticonderoga to sail farther north to provide extra air cover.

Then, early today, the Constellation left Hong Kong with three other warships.

Tonight, President Johnson called leaders of both parties to the White House for a briefing on the latest battle.

News of it was announced just after America had protested to North Vietnam about Sunday's attack on the Maddox.

'TAN THE MODS' SAYS JP

THE Hastings magistrates' chairman, who yesterday sent nineteen youths to detention centres, said last night that he would like stronger powers to deal with hooligans.

The chairman, Mr. Alfred Coote, said:

"It all comes from the steadily-growing indiscipline of the young. It is a pity their backsides cannot be tanned."

Trapped

Mr. Coote, 56-year-old bachelor, said he had himself been trapped in Woolworths when he and other passers-by took refuge there. A crowd of several hundreds was outside.

The anti-Mod police operation at the weekend will probably cost £1,500. Half will be paid by the Home Office.

Local police forces — with Hastings paying the major share — will foot the rest of the bill.

Full court report and pictures—See Page 3.

Michel Jacques, in dark glasses, is helped from the escape shaft—first of the nine trapped miners to be freed.

FOREMAN HERO COMES UP LAST

From AUBREY THOMAS, Champagnole, Eastern France, Tuesday

MAGNIFIQUE! The nine trapped miners of Champagnole were brought back to the sunshine today, after nearly 200 agonising hours in a cold limestone cavern.

The eight days of fears and frustration ended as the hero of the entombed men staggered from the rescue capsule—last man out.

He is Andre Martinet, foreman of the men trapped in a limestone cavern since Monday last week, who volunteered to be at the end of the queue.

Throughout the long "imprisonment," foreman Martinet has kept the men's spirits up by maintaining discipline. The first moment of triumph for the small army of rescuers came at 5.17 this evening.

That was when the FIRST man, 21-year-old Michel Jacques (pictured above, tottered from the capsule into the brilliant sunshine.

He was given a pair of dark glasses, then helped down the steps near the giant American oil drill which bored the rescue shaft, and put in an ambulance.

One by one the other eight followed him up the 270ft. escape shaft, exhausted, groggy . . . triumphant.

They were whisked away

Continued on Back Page

A deliberately cultivated form of modern wickedness, says magistrate

19 SENT TO DETENTION IN 'MOD TOWN'

> This was caused by an invasion of mindless adolescent morons who came here deliberately to make trouble in the hope that they would cause as much noise, damage and distress as possible

—Hastings court chairman Alfred Coote yesterday.

NINETEEN of 32 youths who admitted taking part in the weekend " Battle of Hastings " were sent to detention centres yesterday. And three young men were jailed.

Before he sentenced them, Mr. Alfred Coote, chairman of the Hastings magistrates, said: " This is a deliberately cultivated form of modern wickedness

" There is no reason for this so-called hatred between Mods and Rockers —it is merely an excuse for excitement, thieving and violence."

Mr. Coote said that Hastings had suffered for three days and nights in an appalling atmosphere of tension and apprehension, sometimes amounting to terror.

Trouble

" This was caused by an invasion of mindless adolescent morons, who came here deliberately to make trouble in the hope that they would cause as much noise, damage and distress as possible, and to escape the consequences," he went on.

" We must take into account the overall effect on the thousands of citizens, and on the visitors to the borough."

It was time for Parliament to consider what measures it should take to crush " this form of mass hooliganism, which is apparently repetitive at holiday time," he added.

" If nothing is done, thousands of innocent people will continue to suffer injury, fear and damage to property."

Of the first twenty-one youths who pleaded guilty to offences ranging from threatening behaviour to assaulting the police, ten were sentenced to three months in a detention centre, two were sent for three months and fined £50 with an alternative of an extra three months' detention, three were fined £25, and one fined £10.

Knives

One was sent for six months' detention, another for two terms of three months' detention each.

One youth was sentenced to four months' detention and another to three months with a fine of £25 or an extra three months' detention.

A man aged twenty-one was jailed for two months for kicking in a car headlamp.

All were bound over in the sum of £25 to keep the peace for two years.

When the hearing opened in the morning, police carried a pile of sheath knives and studded leather belts into the courtroom. The accused youths arrived handcuffed together in pairs.

After Mr. Coote announced the sentences, one youth asked if the detention centre to which he was being sent was at Orpington, Kent. He was told it was at Aldington, also in Kent.

As a group of youths left the dock, one whispered: " A cushy old place there !"

At a later sitting three youths were sent to detention centres.

Two men—one aged 25, the other 22—were each jailed for three months.

AT BRIGHTON, one was fined £50 for threatening behaviour on the seafront. Another, aged 17, was fined £20 for carrying an offensive weapon—a beach stone threaded with a thong.

AT MARGATE four youths were remanded on bail until August 26. One was charged with possessing a length of chain as an offensive weapon.

AT GREAT YARMOUTH one of eleven youths charged with threatening behaviour was jailed for three months. The magistrates' chairman said he had a " very bad record."

The ten others were fined between £15 and £40 each.

8 DAYS' CUSTODY FOR JUVENILES

THIRTEEN boys were remanded in custody for eight days when they appeared before a special Juvenile Court at Hastings last night.

Six pleaded guilty, seven not guilty to offences in connection with the weekend riots.

Handcuffed together, two of the youths arrested during the week-end arriving outside Hastings court yesterday. The youths were driven to the building in a coach after a night in custody.

Mr. Alfred Coote, chairman of the Bench.

Dead boy may have been pushed over cliff

James Smart, 14, the Mod whose body was found in the sea.

By MIRROR REPORTER

THE 14-year-old Mod washed up on Hastings beach at the week-end may have been thrown into the sea during a clifftop fight between Mods and Rockers.

And last night Hastings police were looking for the frightened Rocker who saw the fight 300ft. above the beach.

The Rocker says he saw a teenaged boy in Mod clothes flung from the top of Hastings East Cliff after being kicked unconscious in the Sunday-night battle.

Father

The puzzle facing police is: Was this the boy whose body was found on the seashore early on Monday morning?

The dead boy was identified yesterday as 14-year-old James Smart, of Rogers-gardens, Dagenham, Essex.

His father travelled to Hastings after recognising the boy's description in a newspaper report.

The frightened Rocker being sought by police was seen outside Hastings railway station late on Sunday night by 24-year-old clerk Mr. Robert Baird, of Eastbourne.

Mr. Baird said last night: " He was in a terrible state, and looked pale and trembling.

"He told me there had been a terrible fight on the clifftop, and a young boy had been flung over the edge."

Last night Superintendent Kenneth Huntly, second-in-command of Hastings police, said: " We shall be interviewing Mr. Baird and investigating this report.

"We appeal to this teenager who says he saw a fight to come forward and help our inquiries.

" We have had no reports of anyone being flung from the cliff. But if somebody did fall over, it would be quite possible for the body to be washed ashore at the spot where Smart was found dead."

Late yesterday, Hastings police had still not disclosed how Smart died.

Soon after noon yesterday Detective Inspector Osborne Jones, chief of Hastings CID, travelled to Dagenham.

He spent two hours touring the area, talking to friends of the dead boy, who played inside right for the Dagenham schools' football team.

Questioned

Then he went to Dagenham police station.

Less than an hour later, eight boys walked into the police station.

One by one they were taken to an interview room and questioned by Inspector Jones.

Before going in 16-year-old Michael Reid, of Schoolroad, said: " While we were sitting on the beach on Sunday some Rockers came up to us. I told them Jimmy was sick and they went away.

" During the night Jimmy jumped to his feet and said: ' I'm going.'

" I tried to stop him going on his own."

I accept that. Why be a hypocrite? Okay, sometimes I get worried about it but what can you do? The thing I hate most is people in authority, they're idiots, they deserve all they get. I could kill them. I suppose it's because I don't have a chance. I don't talk right and I haven't been to the right schools, I haven't had the education. That makes you sick, to see them preaching to you."

By the August bank holiday the seaside riots had turned into an almost ritualistic undertaking but for now it was just the media that was overreacting. And the law enforcement reaction was as equally outrageous as the press coverage.

The front page of the *Daily Mirror* on August 3, 1964, reported scores of riot police reinforcements being flown Nato-style to the coast to assist in quelling the troubles. And the sentences dished out in their aftermath were designed to make examples of any one arrested, although in most cases that amounted to innocent teenagers who had been rounded up en masse.

'Vermin' says Margate J.P., sending a Whitsun rowdy to a detention centre today. Dr. George Simpson, Chairman of Margate Magistrates said: *"It would appear that you did not benefit from yesterday's proceedings. You were part of the dregs of those vermin which infested this town. As such you will go to a detention centre for three months. Take him away!"*

Possibly the most famous arrest, thanks to its immortalisation in the film version of *Quadrophenia*, was of real life ace face Jimmy Brunton, who upon being sentenced cockily quipped to the judge that he would pay by cheque. Unfortunately, interviewed in the London *Evening Standard* following his release from the cells, Brunton made a rather embarrassing confession: *"The boy who said 'I'll pay by cheque' when fined £75 at Margate yesterday admitted last night "I don't have a bank account". Seventeen year old James Brunton, a bricklayer, was home to a reckoning with his father. Forty-five year old Mr. James Brunton listened in as his son went on 'I thought I could make a little joke. It didn't work'".*

"Mr. Brunton said 'I have no intention of helping with the fine. Jimmy is on his own... we are an ordinary working class family. I just can't understand this business. Today when I took my wife and two younger children down to Bognor I told a neighbour I thought these mods and rockers were no good at all. A few hours later I read that my own son had been fined, I felt

sick and I still do. He has had his job for over a year and he likes sport. Yet somewhere I might have lost contact with him. Then you never have hundred per cent contact with teenage kids these days'".

A psychologist quoted at the time advocated good old-fashioned British common sense: "Teenage rebellion? All my eye. Our memories are short. Mods and rockers are exactly the same nine day wonder as the teddy boys. The best thing is to take no notice".

DRUGS

Drugs and drug culture are as synonymous with the image of Mod as the scooter. The popular theory was that in order to stay awake and dance at the London allnighters, Mods took amphetamine and benzedrine, or any number of these drugs' derivatives such as dexedrine, methedrine or durophet.

Many Mods came into Soho from the suburbs on a Friday night and stayed until Sunday, frequently taking in two allnighters and shopping for clothes and records or making payments on suits by day, simply living the Mod life to its fullest 24-hour capacity.

Alcohol couldn't sustain the level of energy needed for such weekly exertions, especially after a full week's work, so drugs were an obvious option and, it seems, an easily obtainable one.

In 1964, the World Health Organisation (commonly referred to as the WHO, bizarrely enough...) began a survey in which they combined the terms 'addiction' and 'habit' under one heading: 'dependence'. In the survey they highlighted which sections of Britain's society they considered either addicts or abusers. They also reported that the main source of drugs in the inner London area was no fewer than 13 doctors. Given that almost all the known addicts and abusers interviewed for the survey came from London, and Soho in particular, the survey concluded that this area constituted the principal source of drugs for the entire country.

Throughout the course of the survey many Mods were interviewed at length and the findings, along with the names of the doctors, were published in 1965. The Mods were either described as 'the new addicts' or 'the abusers'. These constituted a new type of drug addict, quite different from the earlier, older types, whose origins were deeply rooted in the British jazz subculture, which was very well developed by the mid-Fifties. These were known as 'jazz junkies'.

'H' or 'horse' for heroin, 'c' and 'coke' for cocaine, together with such expressions as 'pad', 'scene', 'square' or 'gig' are described as typical jazz terms, which the survey assumed were gleaned not from direct contact or interaction with actual Americans themselves but from identification through American literature, film and jazz.

The new addicts, however, were described as younger and concentrated in the teenage group. *"Known as Mods, they dress in Mod fashion, either beat or gear, and are abusers of amphetamines rather than heroin or cocaine,"* the survey revealed.

This type of youngster first became apparent around 1960 and was resented by the older addicts or jazzers, one of whom is quoted as having commented: *"They are just a drag, you know, they don't take drugs because of some need or some personal defect. It's just a case of exhibitionism with them, you know, the fact that 'I'm an addict, look at me' type of thing. They go around with long hair and dark glasses, 'the Mod addict', the new crew. They go around with the hypodermic sticking out of their top pocket kind of thing, just advertising the fact they take drugs. These kids, they can go to work in a factory or sell on what drugs they don't use, pay the rent and buy good suits and all the rest of it. Go around with their enlarged pupils, all dressed up and healthy. It's sickening to see, they're bringing the whole thing out into public in a distorted way, so a real junkie who does rely on his daily dose and causes no one any trouble, he's the guy that eventually gets the kick in the backside. He's the one who's going to feel it because of these kids who are rebelling against no-one but their mothers and fathers."*

While that speaker's obvious distaste was for the (negative) publicity that Mods generated over drug abuse, his comments also betrayed a fear that the more drugs and drug use came into the public eye, the more frequent and harder sanctions against users would become. But if he felt that drugs would by implication become harder to get... well, he needn't have worried.

The evidence put forward by an interdepartmental committee on drug addiction, published the same year, stated that *"from the evidence found, we have been led to the conclusion that the major source of drug supply is the activity of a few doctors who prescribe drugs. One doctor alone prescribed almost 600,000 tablets and 6 kilos of heroin. In one year the same doctor on one occasion prescribed 900 tablets to one patient and then prescribed the same patient with another 600 tablets to replace pills he said he'd lost in a road accident. Further prescriptions followed later to the same patient for*

720 tablets and then 840. Two doctors each issued prescriptions for one thousand tablets apiece, while a further six doctors prescribed prescriptions for considerable, if less spectacular, quantities of drugs over long periods of time."

Supplies on such a large scale provided Soho with a massive surplus, yet each doctor was said to have acted within the law and according to their professional judgement. It's not surprising, then, that Mods were known to have the odd packet of pills handy. And the pill of choice was normally drinamyl or, in proper Mod terminology, purple hearts.

Also known as pep pills, purple hearts, so called because of their unique colour and shape, were the most frequently used of all amphetamines. Originally designed for women on weight reduction diets, their association with Mods almost certainly came about via the youngsters' mothers who, it would seem, were in constant supply.

Here are two different accounts of drug use amongst Mods — an early recollection from 1962 and a later account from 1964. Comparison of the two illustrates clearly how rapidly drug use rose in two years.

"We're all aware of drugs and have been from a very early age — purple hearts and marijuana really. We knew that if you went to the allnighter you could buy a joint if you wanted. You could buy joints at the same time you bought your Levi's. All the black guys from the bases used to smoke but it wasn't considered unusual because marijuana was the drug of the jazz musicians. They'd used it for years. Of course the really heavy jazz guys are into cocaine." (In fact one of the earliest known raids in London was on the jazz club, Club II, which was run by the well-respected duo of John Dankworth and Ronnie Scott. Both were busted in late 1950, along with most of the club's clientele; Scott was notoriously charged for possession of cocaine.)

"The black GIs are all smoking joints and taking pills much, much more than the Mods. The Mods have their fiver for a pair of Levi's and that's all they had. The Levi's were far more important that scoring purple hearts.

"The whole thing is being blown out of proportion, in actual fact. The parents are far more outrageous.

There were times when the supply of hearts ran out and then they would nick stuff out of chemists. Anything to turn them on, cough medicine, anything.

All our mothers are on valium or they're on uppers and downers. You think it's all the rebellious young kids but the truth is, the mothers are doing it. My mother, I don't think, has any idea that she's whizzed out of her head. Absolutely no idea she's doing hearts.

"They get them prescribed by the doctor and fly around. My mother would be up in the middle of the night hoovering everywhere and washing and ironing. The next day she would have to be out of the house by seven, to work at Joe Lyons Tea House. Always in catering, my mother. Then every night she would be home with the scrubbing brush. They have to keep going, that's why they're on pills and that's why drugs are so natural to the Mods." (The Stones' song 'Mother's Little Helper', it would seem, was based on fact.)

"You could buy hearts at price ranges from 6d to 1s 6d per tablet. It's very widespread and so easy to get. Marijuana was harder to get but hearts you could always find someone peddling, although you could still end up with some fakes.

"You'd get purple hearts in a little brown packet of ten but you never knew if you were getting eight, nine or ten, or some might be broken up and every little bit counts. You had to open them up immediately to see what you'd got.

"All the Mods that peddled were users who got their supplies straight from the general practitioner but some pills sold illicitly came from thefts and break-ins of factories.

"Unbelievably, there were times when the supply of hearts ran out and then they would nick stuff out of chemists. Anything to turn them on, cough medicine, anything."

Another Mod, Alice, an 18-year-old single white female, describes a typical weekend up West: "On a typical weekend I would leave home early on a Saturday afternoon and go to coffee bars in Hampstead where I'd meet friends. There, we'd get a list of all the parties that would be on that night. We would then go to the West End and other bars to buy our drugs, spend a couple of hours looking for clothes until it was time to go to the first party. We'd stay there for a while before moving on to the next one, then another one and another. At each party you would mix pills with drink and marijuana, then go to an allnighter like The Scene which charged to get in. It had a juke box in the large room with tables and there was a mixture of people, tourists and arty types and a lot of Mods.

"There were two other rooms, one with just benches in it and a smaller room with nothing but planks on the floor, which was used amongst other things for sleeping.

"You never saw anyone taking pills but you knew because they were forever going to get water.

"Everyone would stay there until the morning and regroup at a coffee bar the following lunch-time, in order to get more pills to stop the come down and get you to work the following morning."

Alice was eventually arrested in London for possession of purple hearts and sent to a hostel and then to a private treatment centre, where she and two other female patients managed to abscond in order to visit a chemist and obtain medicines. All three were caught and eventually imprisoned.

MANAGING MODS
Stick with me, son and you'll go far...

As soon as Mod became a mass marketable commodity it wasn't only the high street that took notice; the music industry too smelt rich pickings. There was money to be made from the live music scene in and around London, which was exploding with hundreds of new bands, both professional and semi-professional.

It's well known that on the whole Mods preferred to collect and listen to music made by contemporary US black vocal groups such as The Impressions, The Marvelettes and The Miracles. Motown was in the midst of its first flurry of chart success and American soul stars were beginning to make regular trips across the Atlantic. There were some stars that were already here, such as Herbie Going and Geno Washington, who came to England as American servicemen and stayed on to become Mod soul heroes. Washington in particular became a cult icon in the Sixties.

Mods collected records by these artists as obsessively as they bought clothes. They ignored and derided the charts and absolutely abhorred inferior white cover versions of their precious soul or R&B favourites. Home-grown talent was considered rare, with the exception of Georgie Fame and the Blue Flames and Zoot Money's Big Roll Band who were possibly the only two outfits that clicked with big Mod audiences. This had a lot to do with the distinct bluebeat and jazz leanings of both bands, as well as their allnighter sessions at The Flamingo Club.

However as the Mod movement grew and its influence on British culture began to be felt right across Britain, thanks partly to TV's *Ready Steady Go!*, it was inevitable that genuine 'Mod' bands would eventually appear. These were not a new wave of American soul or R&B revue artists but average everyday British kids fresh from school (well, art school or stage school, anyway) or the shop and factory floor. And all were intent on fashioning out a style and a brand of music and performance that would be uniquely all their own.

The Small Faces and The Who led the charge but there were many that followed in their wake. Not all of them made it but amongst the few that shared the limelight for even the shortest space of time were some of this country's finest and most exciting bands to ever shimmy, shake or power-chord across a stage. Outside The Small Faces and The Who, The Creation, The Action and The Birds were three of the most innovative and exhilarating acts.

Richard Barnes: *"The bands that hit big with the Mods weren't always Mod bands as such. I mean they didn't all look like Mods, sometimes one or two of them were Mod. They went to see any band that played the sort of music they liked, the Mods didn't follow the bands or get any inspiration clothes-wise from hardly any band, they were usually a lot smarter looking than any of the groups on the stage until The Who or The Small Faces but even they had their detractors. I think on the whole the bands that played the big Mod audiences got more from seeing what people in the crowd were wearing. It was totally the other way round."*

Ken Brown: *"The Who, The Small Faces were the big names but also The Rolling Stones. Nobody could really make out what they were. They were a cross between Mods and Rockers — you couldn't categorise them. They were totally individual but they used to wear Mod clothes. You've only got to look at those early pictures and they were wearing bang up-to-date Mod clothes but with really dodgy hair. They never quite got it right but we liked the fact they were individual. Grown-up beatniks!*

"The Who and The Action were the really big bands at my school. The Small Faces, we always thought, were a bit manufactured. They were a great band but we always thought they looked like they were dressed by Carnaby Street, whereas The Who looked like working-class blokes like us in a way... we all know it was, in fact, the other way round and The Who were dressed up as Mods etc., but no one knew it at the time. We thought

The Small Faces were the manufactured group. I knew Keith Moon vaguely, he lived near me in Wembley at 134 Chaplain Road and I was literally just round the corner. My mum and dad knew his mum and dad, so I thought he was just a Wembley lad like me.

"The Small Faces didn't look like everyday street Mods, they looked like pop stars that had been dressed rather than dressing themselves. The Who looked like geezers you would meet down your local, they had street cred. There was this famous story that went round about The Small Faces getting attacked in the café next to the Starlight. They were apparently duffed up by a gang of Mods. I don't know if it was true but that's what everyone used to say."

Whatever the opinion of the Mods on the street, the fact was that suddenly a huge and relatively untapped market had evolved. Live bands were where the smart money was, something that it didn't take long for a few quick-thinking entrepreneurs to work out.

Take Giorgio Gomelsky, for instance. Gomelsky was originally an experimental film-maker whose love of R&B diverted him into promoting and running The Crawdaddy Club at the Station Hotel in Richmond in 1963. This was where Gomelsky put on The Rolling Stones every Sunday night after seeing them play at the Red Lion pub in Sutton. He even became the band's unofficial manager for a short spell, until one Andrew Loog Oldham talked his way into the

band's camp while Giorgio Gomelsky was in Switzerland arranging his father's funeral. Despite his age (he was only 19 at the time) Oldham easily won the Stones over with his charismatic charm and persuaded them to sing up with him for a three-year management contract, signed in an instant by Brian Jones on behalf of the entire band.

Once he had gained his foothold, Oldham, who was pretty much broke at the time, looked around for a sympathetic backer for his new enterprise. His first and obvious choice was Beatles manager Brian Epstein (Oldham had worked for Epstein's NEMS Enterprises briefly as a PR man). Epstein turned the Stones down, thereby blowing his chance of managing the two biggest bands in the world. Oldham eventually found financial stability with business manager Eric Easton.

Fortunately, Gomelsky found a replacement band for the Crawdaddy in another five-piece act, The Yardbirds. This was the band he would preside over from 1963 to 1966, a period that saw The Yardbirds metamorphose from gritty R&B wannabies to experimental pop stars. Gomelsky produced and promoted all the group's releases while they were in his charge. When Eric Clapton, the band's lead guitarist, left in protest over the band's changing musical direction, Gomelsky invited Jeff Beck

GIORGIO GOMELSKY

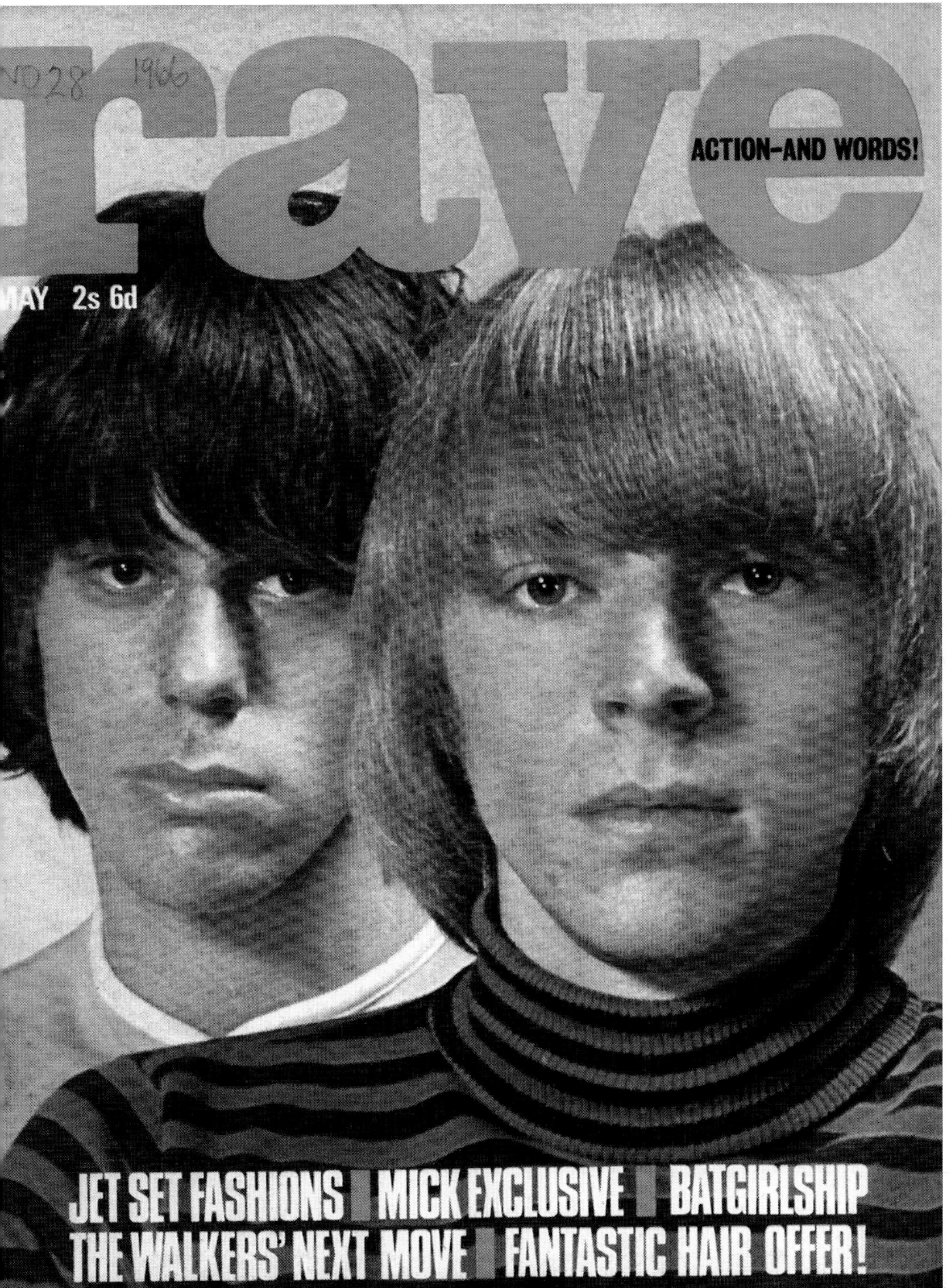

rave

NO28 1966

ACTION–AND WORDS!

MAY   2s 6d

JET SET FASHIONS ▌ MICK EXCLUSIVE ▌ BATGIRLSHIP
THE WALKERS' NEXT MOVE ▌ FANTASTIC HAIR OFFER!

to replace him at the suggestion of Jimmy Page. Gomelsky also managed Brian Auger, Julie Driscoll and the T Bones. His highly individual, hand-written adverts regularly littered the music press, announcing 'Birdmodizing', 'Moddy Boddy Ways' and 'Crawdaddyfying' nights out at the Richmond venue. Gomelsky's almost parental kindness towards all of his young charges became legend in an industry that's not noted for its compassion, unless it involves high-profile charity. Ultimately however, this characteristic came to be seem as a weakness, despite his inventive management and brilliant production work. Gomelsky was often criticised as being incredibly naive, witness the ease with which Oldham had relieved him of the Stones. Yardbirds guitarist and bassist Chris Dreja described Giorgio Gomelsky as *"a rare commodity in the cut-throat world of pop management, a humanitarian."*

But pop stars can be a fickle and mercenary-minded lot as Gomelsky was to find out when The Yardbirds dumped him, this time in favour of the younger Simon Napier-Bell.

'Nice guys always finish last' — isn't that the saying? Well Gomelsky could at least take comfort from the fact that he was not alone. Peter Meaden was another equally enthusiastic pioneer whose creative carcass was picked clean in much the same way. Meaden is still thought of today as the ace face and the sheer embodiment of all that was Mod. Originally a clothes designer for John Michaels, he was one of the first characters to realise Mods hated chart music and hatched a plan to turn the then little-known West London band The Detours, into the capital's first bona fide, albeit manufactured, Mod band.

Richard Barnes: *"Meaden single-handedly turned The Who into Mods for about fifty quid. Meaden had dabbled in a little bit of publicity, having worked briefly for Oldham on some press for the Stones, but what little he had gleaned he put to good use. He took each member of the band and had Jack the Barber trim and comb Mod styles neatly into place. Seersucker jackets, Levi's, two-toned shoes and cycling shirts and a new*

BOYFRIEND

UNDISCOVERED british

IF you haunt the London clubs like the 'Scene' and the 'Flamingo', then don't be surprised if this week's Undiscovered British Boyfriend looks vaguely familiar to you. For 21-year-old Peter Meaden admits he's more often out enjoying the London night life than at home! And this isn't only because he likes the clubs—although that's true, too—but because Peter is one of the behind-the-scene boys in the pop world, and he thinks it's disastrous for anyone in the pop world to get out of touch with the trends. Actually, Peter is one of the people who set them. You've probably heard a lot about tickets and faces lately, well, Peter's a face!

Auburn-haired and blue-eyed, Peter's just a fraction under 6 ft. He was at grammar school and then he left for art school with five 'O' levels and two 'A's to his credit. Art school lasted about one year! Later, Peter had left both school and home for a flat in Hampstead and a job in an advertising agency.

After that—another agency. Then he joined up with Andrew Oldham (the Stones' manager) to form an advertising agency, until last year when he left the country for seven months. After making some money in Spain and North Africa—'something to do with cars'—Peter arrived back in England and almost immediately flew off for a vacation in America for three weeks. He gets around, this boy!

Back from the States, Peter tried his hand as a free-lance photographer and journalist for a while, then finally joined up again with his old partner Andrew Oldham, handling publicity for the Crystals, Gene Pitney and the Stones.

What's next for our Undiscovered British Boyfriend? We doubt if even he knows that! But right now he's a freelance publicist for Chuck Berry and, until recently, for Georgie Fame. On top of that he manages two groups! One is called 'The Moments', the other, still nameless, has just brought out a record! It's called "I Am The Face", and it's penned by Peter.

Being in the pop world, Peter's clothes, as you can guess, are pretty way-out. He buys a new suit every month—favourite of the moment is a black and white checked tweed with back pleat and half belt. And he always wears a very slim tie—no more than half an inch across. Two of his favourites were given to him by Chuck Berry when he came to this country.

Girls for Peter must be very hip. He likes them short-to-medium height with straight, black or blonde hair and tons of eye make-up—including false eyelashes! Face and lips, he likes very pale. And they mustn't take life too seriously.

Because that is something that this Undiscovered British Boyfriend will never do!

Meaden single-handedly turned
The Who into Mods for about fifty quid.

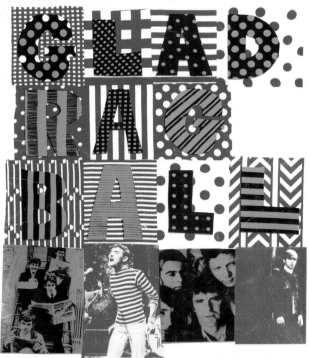

PROGRAMME 2/6

The band had already gained a strong reputation as one of the better semi-professional groups on the London scene, having paid their live due by playing regularly up to three or four times a week. They were led by Pete Townshend whose massive soul and R&B record collection (acquired from a hastily departing American ex-serviceman) was one of the finest outside that of Guy Stevens and the inspiration for much of the band's live repertoire. Meaden introduced the group to even rarer Motown and hatched a plan to break them using his many music business connections and the growing army of Mods.

Richard Barnes: *"Meaden was one hundred per cent cool, he would arrange business lunches at the Oyster Bar in Soho and rave about how big The High Numbers were going to be. He had handouts printed up that proclaimed 'Four Hip Young Men'. He totally believed in it, the whole Mod lifestyle and he was going to project it through the band."*

Guy Stevens' record collection was investigated, along with that of Townshend, for a suitable song to cover. Eventually it was decided that a little bit of selective borrowing was in order. Slim Harpo's 'Got Live If You Want It' became 'I'm The Face' while The Showmen's 'Country Fool' became the flip side, 'Zoot Suit'. Meaden shrewdly took both writing credits. The handout accompanying the release professed, somewhat disingenuously: *"The important thing about The High Numbers which is immediately noted on meeting them is that nothing is contrived or prefabricated about them and this can be said particularly in the field of clothes."*

The single disappeared without trace but Meaden's plan had already started to work. The High Numbers were soon accepted as *the* Mod band, even by the movement's ultra-cool ace faces. Meaden hustled the

He totally believed in it, the whole Mod lifestyle and he was going to project it through the band.

DON ARDEN (FAR LEFT) WITH HIS YOUNG CHARGES BEFORE THE FALL OUT. LORD JOHN, CARNABY STREET, 1965.

group a Scene Club residency and promoted them with some brilliantly placed press snippets, naturally written by himself, including one piece in the girly *Fabulous Magazine* which bragged with breathtaking hyperbole, *"The High Numbers are so up to date they're even ahead of themselves."*

Thanks to Meaden's flawless idealism and resourcefulness the group became scene leaders. But Meaden's catalytic role was to be short-lived. The band, at their own request, was bought from him for a few hundred pounds, by film directors/entrepreneurs Kit Lambert and Chris Stamp. The group changed their name once again, this time to The Who. The name had been suggested some time ago by Richard Barnes and was adopted briefly by the band before they became The High Numbers in the spring of 1964. And the rest, as they say, is history.

A dejected Pete Meaden subsequently turned his attention and somewhat dampened enthusiasm to managing Jimmy James and the Vagabonds and later to publicity for Captain Beefheart. However, bouts of depression saw this Mod maverick spiral into a world of drugs and mental hospitals, resulting in a fatal overdose in August 1978.

Guy Stevens' influence on the musical shaping of the early Mod scene is generally acknowledged as being every bit as crucial as Meaden's. The reputation and sheer size of his record collection may have reached almost biblical proportions today but the importance of his R&B disc nights at The Scene Club remains one of the unanimously acknowledged cornerstones of the movement. His impact was widely recognised by every major artist from the time, bar The Beatles, from The Rolling Stones to The Animals.

Both The Small Faces and The Who credit Stevens for their choices of almost every cover version they did, their inspiration taken from the many compilation tapes that the DJ made at the club. Stevens was also instrumental in pressuring Pye Records into releasing their Chess catalogue in this country in 1964. Moreover, he partnered Chris Blackwell in the running of the Sue

Winston (soon replaced by Ian McLagan), keyboards; Kenney Jones, drums.

He gave The Small Faces an early break by employing songwriters Kenny Lynch and Mort Shuman, whose composition 'Sha-La-La-La-Lee' put the band into the Top Three. Like their first record, 'Whatcha Gonna Do About It', the track was independently produced by Arden for his Contemporary label and licensed to Decca.

Arden knew that 'Sha-La-La-La-Lee' would be a hit – after all, he was paying between £150 and £500 a week (upwards of £6,000 a week in today's money) to have the record hyped by DJs and bought in chart return shops – and it worked.

In the Sixties, the national record charts were compiled by sales from the same three hundred record stores, mostly in and around the London area. This might have made bureaucratic sense, but was obviously easy to fiddle... especially as the identities of these shops could be bought for a mere £5,000, and then targeted by phony customers. Specialist companies were set up to do just that – one such employing four hundred housewives, working for cash-in-hand and part-time, to pose as genuine customers, thus making it possible for a record to achieve a Top Thirty position by selling only five hundred copies in three hundred shops.

Arden was proud of his reputation for being a chart manipulator and rigger par excellence – boasting that: *"all it takes is money to make a star, and I can make a star out of anyone."* Not exactly a new concept in the entertainment industry, and he should have added that many stars were only for Christmas, not for life. Appreciating that an artist might have genuine talent seemed to come a long way down the industry's list of priorities. Rock and pop were considered throw-away commodities, without any real long-term value. Individual bands were to be enjoyed for the moment and then forgotten: another brighter, louder and glitzier one would inevitably turn up. And if it didn't,

record label in the UK, through which he compiled and released ground-breaking collections of tracks by artists including Elmore James, Bobby Bland and Bob and Earl. It's hardly surprising, then, that many regarded him as a vital catalyst in such a new and unique musical climate. Stevens moved into production in 1968 and took on a series of off-the-wall projects including the hippy musical collaboration with Michael English and Nigel Weymouth known as Hapshash and the Multi-coloured Coat. Unfortunately, Stevens was a tempestuous and unpredictable character, renowned for his erratic behaviour and well-known love of the bottle. It was the latter that, after a period of prolonged inactivity during the 1970s (apart from his production of the Clash's seminal *London Calling* album), eventually brought about a fatal heart attack in 1981.

Tales of self-destruction, near-misses and what-ifs were commonplace during this most amazing period of London's musical history. Its vibrant and fresh environment offered opportunities the likes of which had never been seen before, and it wasn't just the charismatic idealists that got wise to it.

Don Arden broke into the pop managerial business with American Gene Vincent. There'd been a brief, Teddy boy rock'n'roll revival in the early Sixties and Vincent had arrived in Britain to try and resurrect his flagging career.

Arden was proud of his reputation for being a chart manipulator and rigger par excellence.

they'd invent one. The idea that a band might possess any sort of staying power, let alone a career, was simply laughable. Naturally, this in no way reflects the current state of the industry: as the Brit Awards prove year after year, hype and short-termism have vanished from the scene, and everyone is now devoted to pursuing musical excellence. Of course they are.

Arden hadn't always seen The Small Faces in this cynical light. In the beginning he genuinely liked them: they made him laugh and they were cockneys, though Arden himself was from Manchester. He'd successfully lured the band away from under the nose of The Who's management team of Kit Lambert and Chris Stamp, aided by Small Faces leader, Steve Marriott. Part of the attraction, for Marriott, was that he preferred Arden's hard-man image to the gentler, more creative Lambert and Stamp. Marriott had also known Arden's son, David, at the Italia-Conti Acting School and the pair had got on well. So Arden seemed like one of their own, mate, aw'right?

To begin with Arden treated The Small Faces well, aggressively promoting the band as a top-of-the-bill act long before they actually warranted it. He opened up clothes accounts for them the length and breadth of Carnaby Street, and the boys were photographed selecting their shirts and trying on jackets. Tales are told of mountains of shirts being delivered to Arden's Oxford Street office, and of how Ronnie Lane refused ever to wear the same one twice. It helped, too, that The Small Faces were short – none of them seemed to top five foot three – and cute, which propelled them on to the covers of girls magazines.

On the performance front Arden turned down lucrative support offers in order to market them as a headline act. He'd also drag the band off TV and radio shows after only one number, in the age-old practice of leaving the audience wanting more, building up the band's mystique and exclusivity. Unfortunately, the band came to believe that they really were the best in the world. They were a good band, very good, despite all the chart rigging, and could have gone all the way but for their aggressive, yobbish attitude which alienated industry insiders and infuriated concert promoters.

Marriott even managed to get the band banned from *Top Of The Pops* after calling the show's producer, Johnny Stewart, a cunt to his face.

Not surprisingly, Arden soon tired of the band's behaviour. On the one hand he admired their youthful bolshiness; on the other, he was in business to make money. He couldn't understand why the band had such a self-destructive attitude to the point of almost wrecking their career before they'd even got started. Publicist Keith Altham, then *New Musical Express*'s most respected scribe, explains it this way: *"They were sort of cheeky, cocky little tearaways, especially Marriott. At first it was all quite infectious and humorous, but it soon wore thin when it never let up. And they never let up, ever."*

Arden understandably grew cold towards the group and began to concentrate on less bloody-minded clients, such as Amen Corner. This caused a rift between him and The Small Faces, with distrust and suspicion creeping in, heightened by the growing concerns of the band's parents over their financial affairs. The band had never seen any accounts or statements, even though

their spending sprees in Carnaby Street were legend. As were the wild, drug-friendly nights at the rent-free Westmoreland Terrace house in fashionable Pimlico. By 1966, they had a driver, a cleaner, and a Number One hit with what many regard as their greatest record, the white soul classic 'All Or Nothing'.

The Small Faces were therefore right to ponder whether they were teenage millionaires, or simply paupers living the millionaire lifestyle. They were only drawing £20 a week spending money, considerably less than bands like The Who or The Action, but £5 more than The Birds, when the band was earning over £1,000 a gig, often playing two separate venues a night. When they confronted Arden, he upped their wages to £60 a week and opened an account for them under the name of The Small Faces. He told the group that all future monies would be deposited into that account – so that was all right, then. Until the parents heard about it and demanded a meeting, which they got, only to be informed – with no little justification - that their beloved sons were taking drugs, and drugs cost a lot of money, and The Small Faces had spent all theirs on

SMALL FACES WITH THE SUPREMES.

clothes, their girl friends, musical instruments and having a good time.

Many years later Ronnie Lane, now sadly dead, explained: *"It took ages to convince our parents we weren't on the needle. It took the attention away from where the money was going. It was still on £60 a week — what sort of habit could you get on that?"*

The situation reached critical mass in October 1966 and the group sought independent advice. This resulted in a legal action, which bogged the band down with court appearances and lawyer's red tape at a point in their career when they desperately needed to deliver a follow-up to 'All Or Nothing'. This was seized upon by Arden as yet one more example of the band's disregard for their career — and after all he'd done for them as well.

Don Arden: *"The record-buying public is notoriously fickle and bands are quickly forgotten if a long gap between releases occurs."* Meanwhile, a rumour reached Arden's ear that Australian Robert Stigwood, a

rival manager and proprietor of the Reaction label, had heard there was trouble in The Small Faces camp and was sniffing around the band. While the idea of getting rid of The Small Faces was undeniably attractive, Arden was adamant that it would be on his terms. This infuriated Arden so much that the self-styled heavy visited Stigwood and, as the myth goes, ordered his minions to hang the hapless Aussie by his ankles out of the window of his fourth-floor office.

Moreover, Arden was astute enough to realise that Stigwood must have been given some encouragement to pursue the band and decided that his cocky little charges must have provided it themselves. So it came as no surprise to Arden when he received a phone call from Yardbirds manager, Simon Napier-Bell, informing him that The Small Faces had been to see him too.
Meetings were held and proposals discussed, but in the end Napier-Bell decided that caution was the better part of valour and decided to pull out of the opportunity. It mattered little as Simon Napier-Bell would go on to manage John's Children, which included former Mod Marc Bolan, and, eventually, Japan and Wham!

American Shel Talmy has gone down producers the business has ever see

So Arden impatiently set his own plans in motion and released a rough demo of the track 'My Mind's Eye', in order to capture the lucrative Christmas market (the song's melody borrowed heavily from the carol 'Angels From The Realms Of Glory). He did so without consulting the band, who then instituted separate legal proceedings against Decca and Arden's own label, Contemporary Records. Sensing a long, drawn-out battle, and bored with waiting for Napier-Bell, Arden finally sold the group lock, stock and legal hassle... to the Harold Davison Agency and Tito Burns, a division of the Lew Grade Organisation.

Arden received £12,000 and bid The Small Faces goodbye. Eventually the group would sign with Andrew Loog Oldham's Immediate label and release their masterpiece, the LP *Ogden's Nut Gone Flake*. Their music also turned away from the Modish white soul towards quasi-psychedelic whimsy, and they enjoyed further big hits with 'Itchycoo Park', 'Tin Soldier' and the unforgettable 'Lazy Sunday'. Alas, their troubles weren't over and Immediate – home also to The Nice, and Amen Corner – was wound up in 1970. Spectacular as their chart successes were, tangible assets in the form of royalties just slipped through their hands like water.

As Kenney Jones later lamented: "It all started when we needed another manager to get us out of the Arden deal and hopefully into a better one. But after the Stigwood business no-one wanted to know — we was to be avoided at all costs. We came to regard the business with Arden as learning our apprenticeship. For years afterwards we would say to other bands 'don't do this, don't do that, learn by our mistakes.' And then there were more problems with Immediate, which left us in an even worse mess, with again no-one wanting to know us."

Arden was later able to prove in court that his company owed the band only the modest sum of £4,023 and seven shillings, accountable up to the June 9, 1967. This was to be paid off in instalments of £250 a month, meaning the

full amount wouldn't be recouped until well into 1969. But following two payments the money ceased. Later, the band instituted fresh legal proceedings, eventually obtaining a winding-up order against Contemporary Records in February 1968. But by this time yet more court cases had left the band almost skint, since Andrew Oldham had dissolved Immediate Records and emigrated to Colombia. They were leaderless too, since Steve Marriott left in 1969 intent on emigrating to America. In the event he formed Humble Pie with another one-time Mod, Peter Frampton, who the previous year had been dubbed 'The Face of '68'.

Few groups in the history of pop drew on their appeal to Mods as heavily as The Small Faces, yet few groups suffered so much through their own naivety and misfortune. The tale brought further tragedy: Steve Marriott died in 1991 in a fire at his Essex home, and Ronnie Lane died in 1997 from multiple sclerosis, from which he had suffered since 1976. Nowadays Ian McLagan lives in Texas and plays sessions, while Kenny Jones got rich after replacing Keith Moon in The Who. Coincidentally, McLagan is married to Moon's ex-wife. In the mid-Nineties Kenny was successful in securing additional royalties on behalf of the group, obtaining a six-figure settlement from the current owners of The Small Faces' catalogue.

American Shel Talmy has gone down in rock history as one of the greatest record producers the business has ever seen. His method was to independently record and produce acts that he'd discovered, and only then license the finished product to a major record company. This ensured that Talmy received the lion's share of recoupable royalties, considered revolutionary in the Sixties, when all recording costs were traditionally paid for by the majors. Talmy was instrumental in developing the unique sounds of both The Who and The Kinks on the albums *My Generation* and *Something Else*, respectively. He also introduced a young David Bowie, then in his Davy Jones & The Lower Third/Mannish Boys period, to the world.

In 1966 Talmy had signed The Who to a five-year production deal, which secured them a contract with Decca/Brunswick on both side of the Atlantic. The Who's managers Kit Lambert and Chris Stamp, the latter the brother of Sixties film icon Terence Stamp, had no idea how to get such a deal, and naively reasoned that Talmy would do it for them. However, panic set in when they realised how much of a controlling interest, not to mention how much in royalties, they'd signed away. Once realisation dawned, they swiftly concluded that Talmy would have to go.

Not knowing how to get a deal in the first place meant that Lambert and Stamp knew even less about getting out of one. There was only person in town who could help them: step up the aforementioned Robert Stigwood, then flush with Cream and The Bee Gees and who (Lambert and Stamp believed) was a multi-millionaire. Stigwood had set up his own label — Reaction — in March 1966, and his first release turned out to be The Who's next single, 'Substitute', which would follow the massively successful 'My Generation', and would be distributed by an eager Polydor. And Shel Talmy would have nothing to do with it. At the very least, The Who hoped to bring Talmy to the negotiating table by such a bold (and possibly illegal) move.

Talmy promptly issued an injunction against Reaction — soon to be Mod favourites The Birds' new label — the moment 'Substitute' came out. Five days later, Decca issue an injunction against Polydor, who were pressing and marketing the disc for Stigwood.

Stigwood retaliated by re-releasing 'Substitute', but this time with a different B-side ('Instant Party', a virtually note-for-note re-recording of the initial B-side, 'Circles', which Talmy had intended to be the band's next single). For legal purposes this meant that it was a different record, and that both Decca and Talmy would need to issue new injunctions. Which they did. The Who reacted by releasing 'Substitute' for the third time, with yet another B-side, an instrumental called 'Waltz With A Pig'. The pig in question was, of course, Talmy, and the track was credited to 'The Who Orchestra', as the band had agreed not to record any new material until the case was heard in court. In fact, The Who Orchestra was The Graham Bond Organisation. In the meantime, with tongue firmly in cheek, Brunswick — Decca's American arm — released the Shel Talmy-produced 'Legal Matter'. The net result of all these shenanigans was that two different Who singles were released within a week of each other, on two separate labels.

As it turned out, Stigwood had overreached himself. The court was less than amused by such a blatant flouting of the original agreement and found in Shel Talmy's favour. He was awarded a five per cent override on all Who records for the following five years. Although no-one knew it at the time, of course, that would include The Who's best-selling albums, including *Tommy*. At the end of the 20th century, The Who's lawyers were still looking for a way to terminate the ruling.

Having lost The Who, Talmy looked around for his next success. Deeply hurt by what he regarded as the treachery shown by Lambert, Stamp and The Who themselves, Talmy turned his talents and attention to reinventing a group called The Mark Four. The latter were a band that Talmy knew had given The Who much of their earlier musical inspiration when both bands played the same London circuit. The Mark Four had just been renamed The Creation by their manager — which to Talmy seemed as good an omen as any. He was determined to make them the biggest band in the world.

As a postscript, The Kinks' 'Waterloo Sunset' refers to Terry (Stamp) and Julie (Christie). This has got nothing to do with Stigwood, Talmy or the Reaction label. But maybe you could do with reminding that the rock world does have its sentimental side.

THE CREATION WITH KIM GARDNER (FAR LEFT).

The Creation were at their gimmicky height in 1966, following two massive European hit records, 'Making Time' and the German Number One 'Painter Man'. The latter was subsequently covered by disco favourites Boney M, who made their name working as session musicians in Germany, in genuine tribute to the pop art Mods that are still legendary today. The problem with The Creation was that they were completely neurotic and terminally paranoid about everything, especially each other. Common practice was for two of the group to gang up on a third and fire him, or for one to quit because he thought he was about to be fired. More often than not they would simply fire each other en masse. This constant conflict made The Creation an anarchic live act and one that taught both The Who and Jimmy Page a thing or two. The Creation was one of the greatest of all the groups that never made it. They were guided by the hand of young American record producer Shel Talmy, who had made his name by successfully recording the pioneering feedback frenzy of The Who.

The band — Kenny Pickett (lead vocals), Eddie Phillips (lead guitar), Bob Garner (bass) and Jack Jones (drums) — had already recorded four singles as The Mark Four. After changing their name to The Creation, they released the brilliant 'Making Time', an angst-filled Mod trash anthem that picked up where The Who's 'My Generation' had left off, on Talmy's independent Planet record label. This was followed by 'Painter Man', a song inspired by singer Pickett's stage act of painting giant action art canvases using aerosol paint cans. Pickett would then use the aerosols as flame throwers with which to burn down the finished masterpiece — and this was over a year before Jimi Hendrix thought about

THE CREATION WITH JACK JONES (SECOND RIGHT).

Constant conflict made The Creation
taught both The Who and Jimmy Page

archic live act and one that
ng or two.

setting fire to anything. Like The Who, The Creation were pop art personified, painting on anything – amps, drums, even naked women.

They would also perform in front of a filmed projection backdrop that showed the band playing live elsewhere, while guitarist Phillips let rip on his instrument (literally) with hacksaws and violin bows (another first). Jimmy Page took note of Phillips' improvisational wizardry and a few years down the line was using a violin bow himself in The New Yardbirds, better known as Led Zeppelin. With good songs, an electrifying stage act, manager Tony Stratton Smith's dogged determination and Shel Talmy's masterful production, The Creation seemed to have all the ingredients a band would need to become a world-class act. Sadly it was not to be. Only a year later the incessant in-fighting had destroyed the group.

Jones had been fired after the second single only to be rehired after two weeks by Pickett who then effectively fired himself, convinced the others were about to sack him (they weren't). He was replaced by ex-Bird Kim Gardner but Phillips then quit under threat of divorce from his wife (she divorced him anyway). He turned down an offer from Townshend to join The Who as a second guitarist and, after a short spell backing P.P. Arnold, became a bus driver. A reassembled Creation featuring Jones, Pickett, Kim Gardner and another ex-Bird, Ronnie Wood, toured Germany in 1968 and released a final single, 'Midway Down'. However, the group's fragile, ever-changing alliances — which paradoxically may have fuelled their hard-edged brilliance — eventually alienated even their most ardent supporters. The Creation finally imploded in 1968. Shel Talmy himself still talks about The Creation as the biggest waste of talent he has yet to come across. Talmy reflects today, *"I never gave up on those guys even after the original band broke up." "They were about to explode in England, they were as good as The Kinks or The Who, maybe even the Stones but they couldn't stand each other. After I moved Planet to Polydor I went to America to get them a big American deal, which I thought would unite them, and I did. I got them a five-album deal with United Artists worth millions of dollars*

THE CREATION, 1966
R: DAVE PRESTON (IN THE BAND FOR ONLY 3 WEEKS!
BOB GARNER, KENNY PICKETT, EDDIE PHILLIPS.

but when I got back there wasn't a band at all, what a fucking waste. Those guys were the biggest regret of my career. When I think of how big they could have been, and they would have been too!"

The Birds fitted snugly in-between The Creation and The Action as one of the country's hardest-working and best-loved live acts. Not to mention being the R&B outfit that got a young Ronnie Wood off his musical starting blocks.

Originally called the Thunderbirds after the Chuck Berry classic 'Jaguar and the Thunderbirds', they were forced to change their name following the high-profile chart success of Chris Farlowe and his outfit, also known as the Thunderbirds. Comprising of the aforementioned Wood (guitar, harmonica), Ali McKenzie (vocals), Tony Monroe (guitar), Kim Gardner (bass) and Pete McDaniels (drums), they formed in the West London borough of Yiewsley in 1964 as a typical youth club band covering contemporary soul numbers, albeit in a distinct British R&B vein. The group built up a sizable local following at their own venue, 'The Nest', actually the Yiewsley and West Drayton community centre, which the band commandeered every Wednesday and Saturday night after winning a local talent contest. This led to gigs further afield at Eel Pie Island, the 'Zambesi' in Hounslow and the 'Cavern' in Windsor.

This was the beginning of a three-year musical journey that would earn The Birds their well-deserved live reputation. For thousands of fans up and down the country, The Birds were British R&B personified. They made several TV and radio appearances, including the Rediffusion spin-off from *Ready Steady Go!* — *Ready*

Group greeted with writs

BYRDS V. BIRDS CLASH IN LOCAL POP ROW

● The West Drayton "Birds" pictured left, are, from left to right: Pete Hocking, Kim Gardener, Tony Munroe, Ron Wood, and Ali Mackenzie.

"As fa concerne Byrds wer — they we prop

WEST Drayton-based pop group, The Birds—stars of the Uxbridge Show—whose record "We're Leaving Here" wa recently in the charts, are in the centre of a major pop music row.

Along with their manager they went to London Airport o Monday morning to meet the American group who recently topp the British hit parade with "Mr. Tambourine Man", the Byrds.

But they were not there in a friendly capacity. Acting m behalf of the Birds an inquiry agent served writs on the five-man American group as they left the Customs Hall after flying in from Chicago at the start of a 16-day visit.

They're using name - say locals

Mr. de Clerck said the British. Later at his London Office

LEO'S
Behind Ex-Service Club Near Rail Station
CAVERN CLUB Windsor
Windsor Berks.

Every Tuesday & Friday Nite
7-30 to 11p.m.

They seek it here   They seek it there
The R & B fans seek it Everywhere

THE BIRDS
Londons newest R & B Sensation
Admission 3/- with this card.

Steady Win — a live battle-of-the-bands contest where they came a dismal fifth out of only six entries, and the BBC variety show *ABC of Britain.* This exposure led to a recording contract with Decca Records courtesy of the famous Dick Rowe, who was still trying to play down his reputation as the man who turned down The Beatles. By the time The Birds came along it seems he had developed a more receptive ear to guitar bands. The group's first single was a Ron Wood original entitled 'You're On My Mind', a steaming slice of harp-driven R&B that showed a maturity in Wood's writing far beyond his young years.

A powerful version of an obscure Eddie Holland Tamla Motown song called 'Leaving Here' followed, giving the band their first and only taste of chart action. The band even got to perform the song live on TV's *Thank Your Lucky Stars.*

The official Birds fan club opened in Hillingdon and the group signed with prestigious agents, the Harold

THE ACTION!

MICK EVANS BASS GUITAR REGGIE KING VOCALS ALAN KING RHYTHM GUITAR VOCALS PETE WATSON 12 STRING LEAD GUITAR ROGER POWELL DRUMS

Marquee Artists Agency Ltd, 18 Carlisle Street, London, W1   Management : Rikki Farr Tel. GER 6601 2 3

invite you at the MARQUEE STUDIO thurs. FEB.10th. 1 p.m. 90 wardour st.

The Action arguably epitomised t

Dances for mods and ROCKERS

A PANTHER PICTORIAL

ON THE SCENE
No.2
2/6

by Marie Cartmell of Radio Luxembourg's DANCING PARTY

Now at last in really easy-to-follow text and step-by-step pictures the way to do the

HUGGY BUG · BOSSA NOVA · HITCH-HIKER CAVERN STOMP · JIVE · BLUES · BEEJE LODDY-LO · HULLY-GULLY · BLUE BEAT TAMOURE

...citement of the London club scene

Davidson Organisation; all the while 'Leaving Here' climbed the charts, and things were looking promising. But in May 1965 disaster struck when the fan club began reporting that hundreds of letters were coming in from angry fans who claimed they were being fobbed off in record stores with a jingly-jangly version of a Bob Dylan tune entitled 'Mr. Tambourine Man'. Yes, the American Byrds had landed. Spelt with a 'y' but pronounced 'trouble'. *"All the fans were being sold their single instead of ours,"* Ronnie explained recently.

The Byrds were billed as America's answer to The Beatles and were about to embark on the year's biggest and most-hyped tour of Britain. The Birds swiftly took legal action in the form of no fewer than seven writs delivered to The Byrds in the arrivals hall of London Airport. The writs claimed the American group had no rights to the name and that the confusion had resulted in the British Band losing substantial amounts of money due to 'Leaving Here' stalling in the charts. The Californians accused The Birds of a cheap publicity stunt and dreamily quoted another of Dylan's lyrics. *"I don't want to compete with you, mistreat you, all I really want to do is be friends with you."*

Undeterred, The Birds quickly picked themselves up and recorded and released a third single, 'No Good Without You Baby' as a follow-up to 'Leaving Here'. The song was yet another great soul stomper featuring The Birds' inimitable aggression, thanks to the twin lead guitars of Wood and Munroe, but alas it would prove to be the band's last pressing for Decca. A switch to Robert Stigwood's Reaction Label brought about a brief name change to the confusing Birds Birds and a final single, 'Say Those Magic Words'. However, due to contractual problems its release was delayed for almost a year. The long lay-off saw the band lose momentum, although tours were booked for 1966. The group also took time out to appear in the cult B-movie classic *The Deadly Bees* with actress Suzannah Leigh, but lack of product, punishing tour commitments and the inexplicable name change had damaged both the band's following and their own morale. Monroe was the first to go, fired by Wood and Gardner, the latter lured away by The Creation, who in turn recruited Wood in 1968. Only McKensie remained, loyally working on The Birds' last recordings, while drummer Daniels simply vanished from the picture. And that was the end of The Birds.

The Who and The Small Faces are the two bands that readily spring to mind when recalling the mid-Sixties Mod scene. However, The Action, an unjustly overlooked five-piece group from Kentish Town, arguably epitomised the excitement of the London club scene far more accurately. The Action started life in 1963 as The Boys, a backing group for singer Sandra Barry, with whom they released a single on Decca; later, a single under their own name came out on Pye. Shortly thereafter the group were spotted by Beatles recording producer George Martin and signed to Parlophone. They released five singles during their two-year life span, between 1965 and 1967, including superlative covers of little-known soul and Motown classics (including Chris Kenner's 'Land of a Thousand Dances', The Marvelettes' 'I'll Keep Holding On' and Martha and The Vandellas' 'In My Lonely Room'), as well as strong originals such as 'Never Ever' and 'Shadows and Reflections'. With The Beatles' producer (and the Fabs' seal of approval behind them) plus a strong Mod following up and down the country, the reasons for their failure to chart remain a mystery. After recording demos for an aborted album, *Brain,* which saw the group exchange their Mod threads for kaftans, they disbanded in 1967.

WHERE HAVE ALL THE GOOD TIMES GONE?

The original Mods, the elitist ace faces of the early Sixties, knew that being a Mod meant far more than simply looking clean, smart and hard. They knew that what they had created wasn't some sort of fad, like the Teds, or a gimmick like the ton-up boys. Mod was an attitude and a belief in a way of life, spawned in direct opposition to the drabness of the real world. That reality meant having to drag themselves up and work nine to five in a thankless environment five days a week, week in and week out, pension, retirement, death. No thanks. Mods had imagination. They saw a brighter future, one in which they would call the shots. They lived in a twilight world of speed, clothes, music (sex was always a lesser consideration) and excitement. They were going to make money and be young enough to enjoy it. So what went wrong then?

Well, to start with, that was only the original vision of Modernism. Once the media got hold of the story, thanks to the explosive Fleet Street coverage of the 1964 bank holiday seaside riots, Mod was effectively finished.

Ken Brown: *"Mod had been a London thing, a street-level secret. Until that weekend, Fleet Street never knew about it, the music papers only barely covered it and then suddenly the whole nation knows about it."*

The media gave Mod to the masses. In doing so they misinterpreted, manipulated and — above all — mass marketed the whole package. As a result it was handed lock, stock and barrel to the high-street retailers as a watered-down and pre-packed version of the real thing.

For a while the movement's founders countered the blatant merchandising of their lifestyles by stepping up their constant evolution. Shirt style, suit styles and haircuts began to change quicker than the life span of a humming bird but they were now slipping out of the hands of the individual — and individualism was what

Mod was all about, after all. The high-street stores had caught up and they wanted control. Specific sartorial statements were their style and they would make them affordable to everyone.

Classic Mod cuts and styles were reproduced in Bri Nylon and drip-dry abundance. Mod, pop and op art imagery was incorporated into the mainstream. Aerosols, hairsprays and cordless shavers were all now Mod accessories. Even scooter dealers got in on the act.

For the originators it was time to go underground once again, leaving their dream to the new pretenders. The new Mods didn't even understand what it had originally meant to be a Mod but, hey, they liked the music, the clothes, the fighting and the drugs. They definitely liked the drugs and they were all going to be faces and oh so modder than thou.

So with the true spirit of Mod all but destroyed in London, we turn our attention to the north.

Mod was an attitude and a belief in a
direct opposition to the drabness of t

of life, spawned in
ul world.

KING OF CLUBS
AN INTERVIEW WITH PETER STRINGFELLOW

"Mods hit Sheffield in 1964. I know because I was already running a club there. I'd started in 1962 with the Black Cat Club, an old church hall. I was 21 and I'd already booked The Beatles. I was booking local bands leading up to the Mod thing happening. Bands like Johnny Tempest & The Cadillacs who were essentially Sheffield's Cliff Richard & The Shadows. All major cities had their version of Cliff & The Shadows.

"Dave Berry & The Cruisers were about the only ones who stood out though. He was playing Chuck Berry music before we knew who the hell Chuck Berry was. Then came The Beatles and Mersey Beat. I booked everything that moved in Liverpool and that's when I booked The Beatles. It was around the time of their first single 'Love Me Do' and it was around the number 17 mark in the charts. Brian Epstein wanted £70 and I said no. We eventually settled on £65 and I thought, 'Number 17, £65, who the bleeding hell are The Beatles? I've promised them £65, no problem, I can cancel them.' And later Brian Epstein rang me from a phone box and said, 'We've got a new one coming out, I think it's got every chance of going in the charts.' He wasn't like 'Hey it's going to be a number one.' Now because they got so busy so quickly they didn't get to me until Feb 1963 and by that time they'd released 'Please, Please Me' and of course it was number one. I had to move the club in to a ballroom called the Azena, named after the owner's wife Azena Fiddle. He was Fred Fiddle and was an undertaker by trade. Anyway I moved it to there 'cos I could sell more tickets and it went very well for me as you can imagine. And I got better, every band I had booked from around the north were doing good business. Bands like The Spider Men, The Undertakers and The Searchers. I heard their record 'Sweets For My Sweet' at the Iron Door Club in Liverpool which was up the road from the Cavern.

"I booked them for £60 and the same thing happened, by the time they got to Sheffield they were number one and we developed from there.

"I opened the Blue Moon Club at the end of a successful 1963 and fuck me if I didn't open with The Kinks, a number one again with 'You Really Got Me'.

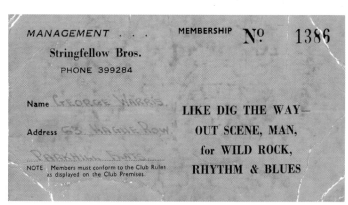

PETER STRINGFELLOW, CLOCKWISE FROM TOP LEFT WITH: GEORGIE FAME, GENO WASHINGTON, BEN E KING AND CLYDE MCPHATTER OF THE DRIFTERS, SMALL FACES, THE YARDBIRDS WITH ERIC CLAPTON.

e they start kicking the shit out
how disc jockeying got started.

I followed that with The Hoochie Coochie Men with the two singers Long John Baldry and Rod Stewart.

"Now we were getting a bit nearer the mark I noticed something was changing. Rod Stewart's hair was a bit of a giveaway. I'd never seen backcombed hair and like everyone else I thought he was gay... this is in 1964 and I started hearing about the Mods in London. The riots had happened and we were getting all these London bands coming up.

"I was doing so well I got offered my own dance hall. A club called Dayze which I jumped at and took over, painted it all black and renamed it The Mojo.

"We caught on to the London scene and called it a blues club, image-wise we happened to catch it all dead right. It only lasted for four years but in those four years we had the whole spectrum of those bands you'd related to the Mods. The Small Faces, The Yardbirds, The Birds... apart from the opening night when I booked a band called Buddy Britain & The Regents. But generally I was getting people like Sonny Boy Williamson, Jimmy Reed, Mike Butterfield Blues Band, they were on the same night as The Animals, Georgie Fame and Geno Washington. They all had big Mod followings by the time they got to me. Geno never had a hit record yet he was the biggest thing playing in Britain. He would pack The Mojo way beyond any other star, he had the biggest and the first Mod following to my knowledge. Georgie Fame did as well but they were a bit more sophisticated.

"Then I started seeing all the younger Mods appearing, the first time I ever genuinely saw it was with The Who. I was very well known as a DJ then, a talking DJ and I got to do the warm-up for a year on *Ready Steady Go!* I still lived in Sheffield but I used to travel to London, do the show and buy records to take back to Sheffield. Stuff that never got played on radio, not even on radio Luxembourg for God's sake, this really was the beginning of disc jockeying.

"I'll tell you how that got started. You've got to understand that when I opened the Black Cat Club way back, records didn't mean a thing, it was all live, who was on. Records were nothing more than fill-in music until the group played again and you would book bands to do three, sometimes four spots, 20 minutes each spot. They'd take a break, you plop these records on and there was no real sound systems then. I mean you could hear the ice-cream van outside better than the records. But it was a start. What I used to do was take the record player, the ones that had the spindle up the middle, put the ten records on and wait for each one to drop. But of course there's that awful gap between each one dropping and I was in a very tough area and every time it went quiet they would start fighting. So I had to get around this every night and I swear to God this is what I did... I took the spindle out and put on a record and then it was a case of how fast I could whip it off and put on the next. Then all I needed was a microphone and talk for a couple of seconds here and there, "that was Cliff Richard and now for the brand new one by..." etc., get the record on before they start kicking the shit out of each other. That was how disc jockeying got started. Anyway back to the story...

"I used to go to this cellar underneath the Whisky A Go Go (The Flamingo) on Wardour Street, in 1965 and this American guy that sold records every Saturday night. Now you never heard them or even knew them but you bought as many as money would allow and take them home hoping you had some good ones.

"*Ready Steady Go!* did a Northern Special, Herman's Hermits, The Big Three, and they wanted a northern DJ. I got patronised like crazy by the southerners. A lot of Mods had come down from Sheffield and I took them all out to a club, The Scene, afterwards. A load of East End hard-nut Mods were in the club — we lasted ten minutes before I had to get all these wimpy Sheffield Mods back on the coach! They would have killed us."

THE STRINGFELLOW BROTHERS WITH SONNY BOY WILLIAMSON.

CITY HALL (OVAL) SHEFFIELD
TUESDAY 18th. MARCH
ONE SHOW ONLY AT 8 P.M. (doors open 7·30)
STRINGFELLOW BROS.
PRESENT
IN CONCERT II
FLEETWOOD
MAG
AND
MICK ABRAHAMS
BLODWIN PIG PLUS THE VILLAGE
Seats 15!· 12'6· 10!·
Tkts from Wilson Peck & Cann Broadway Sheff

AZENA BALLROOM GLEADLESS
SATURDAY 12th FEB. 1963
Live! ON STAGE
FROM THE CAVERN CLUB
THE
BEATLES
No.1 Single
"PLEASE PLEASE ME"
Presented by STRINGFELLOW BROS.
Tickets 6!· OBTAINABLE FROM THE BLACK CAT CLUB

THE KINKS AT THE BLUE MOON, 1963.

ast End hard-nut Mods were in the club —
e lasted ten minutes before I had to get
l these wimpy Sheffield Mods back on
e coach!

I WAS A TEENAGE SMALL FACE
AN INTERVIEW WITH KENNEY JONES

"I remember walking just round this corner here (Mile End Road) and I saw... it was the first Mod attack, really. There must have been maybe four Mods coming out of the Italian and this one guy had cuban heels on, they were like Mexican dancing boots and that's what got me into Mod, just that one bloke.

"Before that I just remember growing up in black and white until I became a teenager and I remember coming up to, I think it was called John Reid's or something like that. I bought the very first Caramel jumper, it was lovely. They made them in different colours. Three button down to there, extended collar, you know the style, Paul Weller wears them all the time. And white Levi's, which was the major breakthrough... I was probably 13... just before I played the drums. And we used to rampage up and down Roman Road towards Victoria Park, that used to be a Mod hang-out. We used to sit on the grass and there were... like, sections of Mods everywhere. All the birds used to go there and that was the attraction... If there was a chocolate machine or a cigarette machine or anything like that we used to rip it off the wall and God knows what. Terrible, actually. We used to get to Victoria Park, always (in) the summer as I remember, and we used to get the boats out on the Lido because it wasn't very deep and we used to tip people up. In our white Levi's... we never used to take them to the dry cleaners because they were sacred, you know. We used to like to show our socks, basically. I think it was because we didn't know quite where to stop the leg or the trousers used to shrink, one or the other.

"When I was at school I used to go up to the West End and hang around Soho. I nicked a scooter. My first public appearance was in young offender's court because I nicked a scooter with some mates. It was a light blue Lambretta and the clutch had gone, so I repaired the clutch. And I chromed the panels and I jazzed it up and put lamps on. It was in shitty nick and I turned it into brilliant nick! Then me and my mates were playing on it, driving round the corner and the Old Bill pulled up. They knew it was nicked because we hadn't changed the number plate. Anyway, this little old boy got it back in absolute superb condition, so I don't feel too bad! I used to see people like him all the time. When they first came over they were like one step up from a moped. Imagine somebody... a 65-year-old man on a basic Lambretta, that's how scooters were viewed at first, old men's commuter bikes. That's why we jazzed them up, to stop them looking boring.

"I have never ever owned a Lambretta since. I used to ride loads of them with my mates, but I didn't play drums then and was in a different frame of mind. And I was too young to have a scooter license or a driving license. The minute I got my driving license I got a Mini, which I call the official Mod car, you know. I'm more of a Mini man than I am a scooter man. I had one with black-and-white check painted on the bonnet and the roof. I've got a Mini at the moment, it's a Mini Cooper. I've got black windows in it and all that shit. I was thinking of putting the black-and-white checks back on the roof and bonnet of it.

"There was a lot of jealousy on the Mods' part when The Small Faces got big. No-one went off us, we did go a little bit up-market, because you would do. The only way we could get any money out of anyone was... we had accounts with shops in Carnaby Street. I'd go up there and buy six shirts at a time. My Mini was like a clothes shop, you know. You'd wear this stuff and take it back and get the money back. Carnaby Street had exaggerations of our Mod stuff really. I suppose because we had more money than the average Mod we could buy a bit more, but then we needed it because we were on TV, that's what caused it. And we were influenced by other people in a sense. But in the main, what we wore every day, as you can see in photographs, was Mod. If there was a lot of resentment, it was from the fact that all the girls used to scream and shout and it used to piss the Mods off who used to come to watch, seeing their girlfriends scream at us. That went on for a few years until about 1966. But Mod was dying out by then and flower power was coming in but we were still definitely Mods in 1966.

I tell you what killed the Mod, the cra

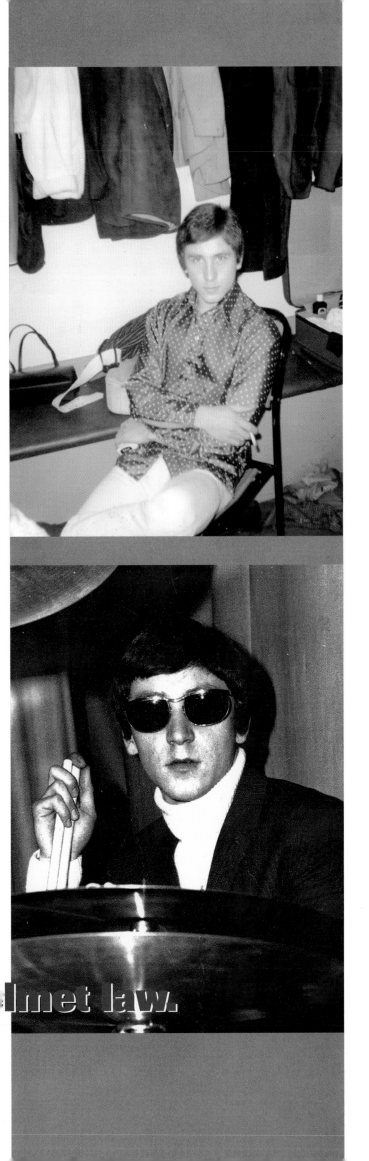

"I tell you what killed the Mod, the crash helmet law. When they brought that law in, there was a big hoo-ha, I remember, everyone was up in arms because the Indians could wear turbans instead of the crash helmet and we said 'Well fuck it', you know, 'we can't have that.' To be honest, a Mod looks absolutely stupid with a crash helmet on. I used to have a little French beret and that would sit forward, nice, perfect. I was a bit pissed off myself... one of the great things was, you didn't have to wear a crash helmet, it wasn't a legal requirement, and mainly because of the Mod hairdo it was perfect. If you put a fucking crash helmet on it would kill your hairdo, wouldn't it? It kills the old Mod look stone dead... that's my opinion, anyway. Plus, everyone had got a tiny bit older and had a girlfriend and the girlfriend was probably on at them to get a car — 'I'm not getting back on a fucking scooter.' Fantastic era, though.

"The riots were just a one-off thing that didn't help. There weren't that many riots, there were small clashes, especially around Forest Gate, The Lotus in Forest Gate — that was a real Mod hang-out. Mod became a fashion statement in the end after the riots but the Mod thing never stopped happening really. It went up the north and back into clubs.

"I went to a few, I went to the early ones. They were great, they did away with all the old music. All there was on before Mod clubs was, do you know what I mean, 'Runaway' and things like that, old songs. They were great places, very good actually because what it was, was the Hush Puppies and the plastic macs, white Levi's and people generally having a fucking good time.

"The Rafton on the corner of Bethnal Green Road was a good club and then there was the 58 Club, Hackney. It was like a town hall sort of thing. I saw a lot of bands there. The Gladiators, that was very popular, a lot of Mod bands like The Action.

"The Who were Mod, and we were Mods. In the press we were 'rival Mod bands'. It's like that thing with Oasis and Blur. I don't know if they really are, but that's what always gets printed, like us and The Who. We weren't rivals, it was mutual appreciation. Did you know Roger Daltrey was a sheet metal worker? That's why he's got big hands. That's why he always catches the mike, that's what he says anyway."

READY STEADY GO!

Back in the summer of '63, just as The Beatles were whipping Britain's jaded music scene into a frenzy, *Ready Steady Go!* was launched as the nation's first foray into what is now known as 'yoof TV'. Prior to RSG!, music on television consisted of charming but uncomplicated programmes such as BBC Television's *Juke Box Jury,* which featured a format that still resembled the Fifties! But RSG! came to the rescue. With 175 programmes spanning the next three years, and its slogan 'The Weekend Starts Here', it came to epitomise the Swinging Sixties, thrusting home-grown talent such as The Beatles, The Rolling Stones, The Who, The Hollies, The Kinks and The Small Faces, amongst many others, into Britain's living rooms, as well as importing cool American sounds such as Otis Redding and The Byrds.

With resident hosts Keith Fordyce (formerly of another ITV pop show, *Thank Your Lucky Stars*) and Cathy McGowan, you could groove to the latest, Mod-est dance craze, pick up hot fashion tips, and generally make a fool of yourself in mime competitions. RSG! went out at tea-time on Friday evenings. The première edition featured Billy Fury performing 'In Summer' and 'Somebody Else's Girl' alongside Brian Poole & The Tremeloes, who performed 'Twist And Shout' and 'Do You Love Me'.

No artist ever made a fortune on the programme. For their rendition of 'Bus Stop' on July 1, 1966, The Hollies were paid a handsome sum of £47/50 shillings, and for 'A Girl Like You' on August 5, The Troggs received 50 shillings more! But more importantly, the show often made pop history. The episode transmitted on December 16, 1966, featured the TV debuts of both Jimi Hendrix (with his Experience) performing 'Hey Joe', and one of Marc Bolan's earliest performances with 'Hippy Gumbo'.

The final edition was transmitted, with the aptly amended title of *Ready Steady Goes!,* at 6.08pm on December 23, 1966, featuring an (almost) Who's Who of popular music from that time. Dave Dee & Co, Eric

CATHY McGOWAN, THE FACE OF READY STEADY GO!

THE VARIETY CLUB OF GREAT BRITAIN WITH THE CO-OPERATION OF **REDIFFUSION** WELCOME YOU TO THE **READY, STEADY, GO!**

EMPIRE POOL, WEMBLEY
WEDNESDAY, APRIL 8th 1964
7-30 to 11-30
OFFICIAL PROGRAMME

1/-

ALL PROCEEDS TO CHILDREN'S CHARITIES
THROUGH THE VARIETY CLUB

Burdon, Alan Price, The Who, Mick Jagger, Chris Farlowe, Lulu, two of The Yardbirds, Paul Jones, The Spencer Davis Group and Donovan were among the featured artists to see out the Sixties' finest pop programme.

Sadly, only three complete episodes survive in the 'Official' Dave Clark (of Dave Clark Five fame) archives, two of which feature The Beatles. There are also many 'insert' performances and 'off-cut' clips (sent abroad, but never returned, e.g. The Walker Brothers from 1966, which I personally found in German TV archives, and which have since been returned to Mr. Clark). When Rediffusion lost its franchise (ending its right to broadcast on ITV) to Thames in 1968, the company moved into television rental and vacated its Aldwych HQ in the city of London. A cache of videotapes (then highly prized for their reusable value), possibly

including episodes of RSG!, were apparently donated to the up-and-coming Filmfair company for them to record their new *Magic Roundabout* series on. The remaining archive was loaded onto a van, but spookily, never arrived at its destination. The old building has since become the registry for births, marriages and deaths; there's even talk of a cover-up in which the entire collection continues to exist, but is currently hidden away in a secret government warehouse, owing to its supposed inclusion of 'delicate' material.

The entrepreneurial Dave Clark bought what was left of the RSG! archive, apparently found underneath a stairwell of the old Aldwych site. Everything that has been seen on the PMI home videos and the Channel 4 compilations (in England) and 'Disney Channel' compilations (in America), stems from that hoard. But there is still much more that has yet to be recovered!

THE YARDBIRDS WITH JEFF BECK.

By Appointment
To H.R.H. The Duke of Edinburgh
Manufacturers of Vespa Scooters
Douglas (Sales & Service) Ltd.
Bristol.

THE VALUE-FOR-MONEY SCOOTER

SCOOTERS
Your first-class ticket to independence...

The most enduring image associated with Mods must surely be that of the Lambretta or Vespa scooter. Originally a pioneering British invention, the scooter was abandoned and eventually (like so many great British inventions) perfected and imported back from the Continent, this time from Italy.

The scooter was 'the' Mod accessory, a mode of transport that set its rider apart from any conventional uniformity or mobility (well, to start with anyway). A clean, neat and curvaceous machine that awarded Mods the freedom of travel while eliminating the inconvenience of rubbing shoulders with the general public. Yes, for the Mod the scooter was the obvious choice.

It was neither big nor cumbersome and with the engine totally encased and hidden the rider stayed clean, unlike the rider of a motorbike. Not that Mods tinkered with engines – that was considered totally uncool. They were easily available too, coming along at a time when England was introducing and experimenting with the hire purchase scheme, whereby weekly repayments meant it was simple to own almost anything, even a brand new bike.

Italy had been building scooters since the mid–Forties, turning them out in their thousands from factories rebuilt using the Allied money that poured into the country after the war.

The demand was so great that they became one of the country's biggest exports and almost single-handedly restored the country's engineering industry.

Being Italian-built suited the Mods philosophy down to the ground and it gave the scooter that extra appeal that they loved. The bike's sleek lines and bosom-like curves (on the Vespa, anyway) also gave the bike an almost feminine quality that, when individually customised, accentuated each bike and rider's individuality. This made customising an important factor in itself.

Customising scooters was made easy by the sheer amount of accessories and additions available at the time, from scooter outlets like 'Eddie Grimsteads' in Barking, 'Woodford Scooters' or 'Scoot-a-long' on the Old Kent Road.

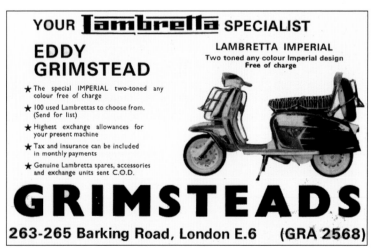

NEWHAM DRUIDS SCOOTER CLUB

FORESTERS VESPA CLUB WANSTEAD

EAST LONDON ELK LAMBRETTA CLUB

THE RAKES EPPING FOREST LAMBRETTA CLUB

KENSINGTON SCOOTER CLUB

MORECAMBE RALLY 1967

Castrol

Car lights such as jag lights were added to the back panels, which incorporated extra stop or parking lights. 'New Yorker' or 'Florida' bars would also encircle the panels and thus gave the bike extra protection were the rider to drop it.

A rack would sit on the front and this would be adorned with more lights, mirrors, alpine horns and mascots such as the Rolls-Royce flying lady or the Jaguar's leaping big cat.

All these extras would, of course, slow the bike down considerably, although this didn't bother Mods, as speed of the 'accelerating' kind wasn't a priority. The slower you went the more people saw you and Mods weren't shy of being seen or known.

Ken Browne: *"You would always put your name on the flyscreen, above the headlight. Kenny Wembley or John Ealing or whatever. That was a big thing. You could buy little stick-on letters, either plain or reflective and you would also have it on your parka plus, and here's something I've never seen a photo of, Mods would put the engine size on the back of the parka. If it was an Li 150 or GT 200 or GS 160 or whatever, you put it on, for some reason. That was big in Wembley. If you had a parka it was compulsory.*

"I don't think I knew anybody who didn't have a parka that wasn't covered in graffiti. Band names too, Small Faces or The Who, you'd have the lot on there. Although most of the photos I've seen were taken at Brighton during the riots and I think a lot of that stuff came after that."

One of the big selling points on scooter sales literature was that scooters offered foul weather protection, courtesy of the leg shields. This, of course was nonsense, as the shields offered little to no protection, and only made the bikes difficult to ride competently.

You would always put your name on t headlight. Kenny Wembley or John Ea That was a big thing.

FOREST
GATE
CHESTER

screen, above the
r whatever.

Graham Hughes: *"There was a correct way of riding. You stuck your feet out at an angle of 45° and if you had a pillion on the back, he would sit with his hands behind his back and lean backwards."*

The Vespa's engine was to the right of centre, counter balanced by a spare wheel (which didn't counter balance it at all) and hidden by a bubble panel, which led to difficulties when cornering, especially in the wet. On the other hand, the Lambretta's engine was centred in a steel tubular frame and encased on both sides by a more streamlined panel. This made it less accessible than the Vespa's and vibrated the entire bike, which became a problem when adding accessories, as anything bolted to them eventually fell off.

Many of the Lambretta's parts are also interchangeable throughout the range of models, which makes it hard to buy, for instance, a genuine TV 200 today in its original state. Although I have it on good authority that to the untrained eye, it would look spot on.

The Lambretta TV 200 was a much-favoured bike with a lot of Mods, a sleek, almost rocket-shaped dream of a machine. It was the first to come in a whole range of two-tone colour schemes by way of the panels and mud-guards.

The panels would fit flat either side, fastened to the frame by a knuckle closer and finished with aluminium flashes that were meant to give the impression the bike was moving even when stationery.

There was a correct way of riding. You stuck your feet out at an angle of 45° and if you had a pillion on the back, he would sit with his hands behind his back and lean backwards.

The TV was also the fastest production line scooter made, capable of clocking up an impressive 75 miles per hour, which put it literally miles ahead of its nearest Vespa rival, the GS 160.

The production and performance rivalry between Lambretta and Vespa was extremely fierce during the 1960s with both companies constantly striving to outshine and outsell the other in what was a very lucrative market. Sales figures published in 1965 showed scooters outselling motorbikes by three to one – obviously not all to Mods, although they were the bikes' main procurers, either legally or otherwise.

Stories of scooters being stolen were common and widespread. Security, it seems, was very low on the manufacturers' priority list. For instance, the same ignition key started all Vespas made between 1956 and 1965 and the Lambretta's knuckle closers weren't lockable. This made it very easy for Mods to steal bikes from other areas or from opposing gangs, and replace engine parts or damaged panels.

As the race to perfect both Lambrettas and Vespas intensified, new top-of-the-range models were created with each successive bike intended to update and replace the last. This was in keeping with the Mod ideal, of which two essential ingredients were the need to be quick off the mark and bang up-to-date. This consequently meant only the newest top-range scooter was considered and no other was good enough for boy or girl.

Ken Browne: *"If you met a girl in a club you fancied you would wait to make your move, always at the end of the night. You didn't want to get involved any earlier, for fear of spending any money on her. You were basically interested in taking her home, so you'd ask if she wanted a lift and she would actually ask you 'What scooter have you got?' You'd have to say you had a GS or a GT 200, because they knew they were the ones to have. Boy, if you said it was a LD 150 or whatever you had no chance. There were scooters that were totally passé, like the LD and the Sportique, you just didn't want one of those.*

"It would have to be a GS or GT or, at the worst, a TV 175 or even an Li. Girls knew about it, if they were up on it. They'd turn to their mates after and say 'I'm going home with him, he's got a GS' and that would be it. You'd get them on the back and drive some place, bonk them down an alley, if you were lucky. It was a bit difficult bonking on a scooter... but I tell you, they actually knew what was what."

The earliest top-flight scooters according to Mods were the GS 150 and the TV 175 series two, which were replaced in 1962 by the GS 160 and TV 175 series three. The latter was succeeded by the GT 200 in 1963 and then by the SX 200 in 1966. The GS 160 was in turn superseded in 1965 by the SS180 and all were considered the scooter to have in their respective years, depending on whether you owned a Lambretta or Vespa of course.

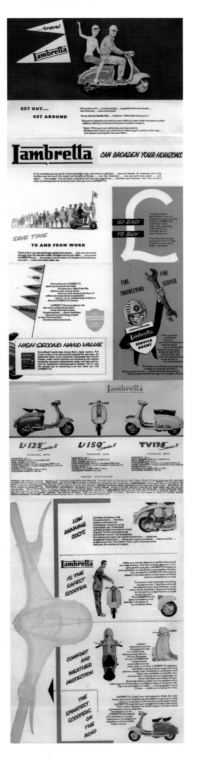

The debate over the relative merits of owning either a Lambretta or Vespa has raged on for years and shows no sign of abating even today, with the benefit of hindsight. The reality in the Sixties however, was that decisions on purchase were rarely made over an objective assessment of each make's technical advantages. It simply came down to personal taste, whether a Mod preferred the look of a Lambretta or Vespa and like supporting a football team, very few were ever won over by the rival make.

Ken Browne: *"The Vespa GS 160 was the ultimate London Mod machine. It was only available for a couple of years, between '63 and '64. Bob Strutton was the ace face around Wembley, him and another guy called John Windows. Strutton would hang out at a club called The Pendulum, which was a little Mod club out that way, and he had a GS 160, which had a lot of chrome and mirrors and I thought it was just mind-blowing. Then there was The Starlight Club, where Windows hung out and he had a GT 200 which was all chrome, apart from yellow panels and one yellow flash. Every other bit of it was chrome, even the frame. He was very ahead of his time, he had the blonde hair and looked exactly like Sting in* Quadrophenia. *That character could easily have been modelled on John Windows and he actually became a dustman. Those two guys were the faces in Wembley and, of course, they had to have opposite scooters and each swore theirs was a better model. But on the whole most Mods I knew had, and preferred, Lambrettas"*.

The Lambretta was the most popular of the two bikes for two reasons. Firstly, there were simply more Lambretta dealers than Vespa, and secondly, the Lambretta was better marketed than the Vespa.

Vespas were both imported into Britain and built here, under license to the Bristol-based firm, Douglas. Douglas only built the Sportique model in the UK and imported the rest, including the GS, from Italy.

This made the Sportique their number-one priority and the scooter that the factory profits depended on. Consequently, nearly all of Douglas' advertising featured that bike and practically ignored the GS.

FLEXIBILITY PLUS

The Sportique 150 c.c. rotary valve 4-speed model ha[...]
progressive two stroke engine ever designed. Its extr[...]
will be welcomed by those who travel in heavy traffic[...]
... The enthusiast will appreciate its brisk accele[...]
smooth performance, whilst those who have an eye[...]
day running costs will benefit by the all round perform[...]
Technically, the Sportique is a masterpiece of e[...]
precision and incorporates everything that has made[...]
name in scooters.

All Sportique riders were ritually an
the older Mods who, it seems, rode
the Sportique.

Lighting:
Headlamp Main Beam, dip, speedo and tail light by A.C. from 6 pole Magneto, Parking lights and horn from D.C. Battery.
Ignition:
Flywheel Magneto with external H.T. Coil.

erall height:
ins.
weight:
lbs.

Gear Box:
No. of Gears: 4.
Ratio 1st   13.35 : 1
2nd   9.32 : 1
3rd   6.64 : 1
4th   4.73 : 1

TECHNICAL SPECIFICATION

Bore:
57 mm.
Stroke:
57 mm.
Capacity:
145.45 c.c.
Compression Ratio:
6.5:1.
Power:
5.5 b.h.p at 5,000 r.p.m.

Wheels:
Interchangeable 3.50 x 8.
Max. length:
68.7 ins.
Max. width at Handlebars:
27.9 ins.

lessly derided by thing other than

The Sportique was a fine little commuter bike. It had a low-revving, ultra-reliable engine, small frame, tiny eight-inch wheels and was ideal for manoeuvrability in heavy traffic. Good features, but all together too conservative to catch the imagination of the Mods' buying eye. They felt the bike lacked any real style and called it an old man's scooter. Realising this, Douglas introduced a range of Sportique special editions,

specifically aimed at the Mod market. These new bikes offered ready-chromed panels and a metallic paint finish and perfectly illustrated just how little Douglas knew about Mods' hatred for blatant commercialism and their passion for individualism. However, the little bike did sell to the younger, uninitiated Mod and in enough numbers for it to be considered successful.

Successful for Douglas, at any rate. The purchasers themselves, however, soon grew to regret their choice, as nearly all Sportique riders were ritually and ruthlessly derided by the older Mods who, it seems, rode everything other than the Sportique.

There were two clearly defined categories of acceptable accessories: cool or uncool.

Now the Lambretta importers on the other hand, experienced no such problems. Since they had no factory or production line overheads to worry about they could concentrate solely on importing and marketing Lambretta's entire range of bikes, with brilliant and enthusiastic promotion campaigns that were effective, stylised and above all, successful.

Contrary to popular belief the art of customising scooters didn't originate with Mods. Nor did it start in the Sixties.

Customising had started almost as soon as the bike was invented back in the early Fifties, with the formation of Vespa and Lambretta clubs and race meets. These scooter enthusiasts would arrive with their bikes gleaming and sporting white wall tyres, crash bars, front racks and wheel discs. Mods took it one step further.

There were two clearly defined categories of acceptable accessories: cool or uncool. In the cool department, were items such as small flyscreens, crash bars, chromed front and back racks and leopard skin seat covers, whereas uncool additions almost certainly were flags and pennants, panniers, chrome portholes, painted racks and worst of all, large plastic screens with a letter box cut out. Looks for scooters changed just as frequently as fashion in clothes did, but generally speaking there were two main looks. First came the chromed look. This started off with just the side panels and gradually spread to every part of the bike that could be detached, such as the mud-guard, fly wheel cover, cylinder cowling and glove boxes.

The spotlight and mirror craze lit
winter months of 1963 and 196

Lambrettas, with their bolt-together construction, had the best chroming potential. They featured detachable head set tops, horn casings and even leg shields.

Mods didn't like to be kept waiting for work to be done on their bikes, so dealers started an exchange service, which covered resprays as well.

Resprays were as popular as chroming and could be very expensive, especially if the main body of the scooter was resprayed. The most desired effect, for a while, was dark colours with chromed side panels. This looked particularly good as most Vespas' and Lambrettas' bodies came only in white.

Despite the expense of chroming, most of the work was of a dismal quality and nine times out of ten the chrome would completely fade well within a year, but hey! Mods were about living for today, so complaints were presumably few.

Another popular look was two tone. This enabled the bike's appearance to be dramatically altered for a smaller financial outlay, as only parts of it – panels, horncasings etc. – would be sprayed.

This was one of the few conversions Mods could do themselves, thanks to the relatively new arrival of multi-coloured aerosol cans.

The spotlight and mirror craze literally erupted during the winter months of 1963 and 1964, and it reached its peak that same summer. Due to the bulk of photographs being taken during the Easter bank holiday riots of 1964, this is the image that's come to symbolise the whole Mod scooter phenomenon. This entire image, however, was completely outmoded by the end of the same year and replaced by the back to basics approach.

erupted during the it reached its peak hat same summer.

UN NUEVO MODELO DE LINEA MAS DEPURADA
Y MECANICA INCOMPARABLE

Dotada de nuevo motor, más potente 7,6 HP y con mayor reprise que alcanza los 97 km/h., arranca siempre, fácil y seguro. Suspensión delantera basculante y posterior con amortización. Chasis de tubo indeformable. Frenos de expansión. Faro monobloque de gran potencia con cuenta-kilómetros incorporado... etc. De línea estilizada y actual «más cómoda para el pasajero» y manejable para el conductor. Color plata metalizada y acabado impecable... Es el vehículo ideal para circular con rapidez por las grandes ciudades, y correr con seguridad por cualquier carretera.

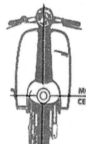

MOTOR CENTRAL

Lambretta
LA SCOOTER QUE DURA MAS

1 año de garantía

SCOOTERLINEA 125

SCOOTERLINEA 150

SCOOTERLINEA 175

150

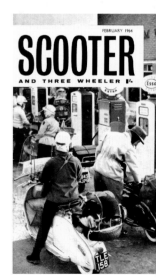

There were several other lesser trends that came and went as well, such as the skeleton look that also emerged at the tail end of '64 and which was possibly a reaction against the earlier excess of lights and mirrors.

This trend involved removing as much of the body work as possible and was a look limited to Lambrettas because Vespas had non-detachable bodywork, although, there was a period when Vespa riders ran GSs and SSs without their side panels. This allowed the side-mounted spare wheel to be exposed and embellished with a wheel disc, and a white wall tyre. Unfortunately, this left the electrics exposed on the other side and after a few breakdowns caused by a wet ignition coil, the panels eventually went back on.

Another style was the street racer look. This had a limited but enthusiastic following from around 1963 onwards and was about the cheapest effective form of customising.

The bike was very rarely sprayed because the rider relied on electrical or reflective sticky tape to alter the bike's looks. Tape was applied in twin narrow stripes that ran vertically down the leg shields and over the panels broken up with a race competition number, *Herbie Rides Again* style. It was later discovered that this was, bizarrely, illegal and the numbers were removed and a white roundel left in their place.

Other aspects of this style included a wire mesh guard over the head lamp and spot lights bolted directly on to leg shields protected by black-and-white check racing covers.

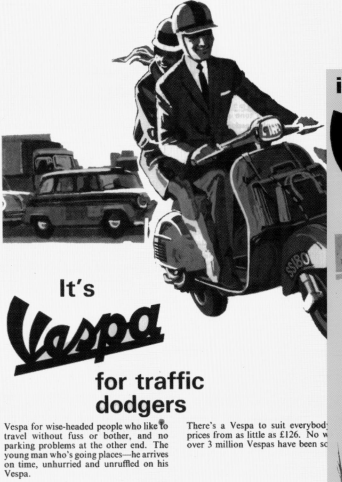

Not all customising trends worked – copper plating, for example, or painting over chrome. All-over murals were another fad, although this was taken on up north and later became very popular.

By 1966 the definitive Mod scooter had fully evolved and for once Mod meant moderation. This style took a little bit of all that had gone before and applied it subtly, a couple of spot lights mounted either side of the crash bar, fly screen, a pair of head set mirrors, rear rack and if the scooter was a Vespa, jag lights or chrome panels.

And all this needn't even be done by the owner because by '66, ready-customised scooters were on offer from individual and reputable dealers like Grimsteads who had The Grimstead Hurricane, Vespa GS or the Imperial Lambretta SX. There was also a Woodford Z type and even a Motobaldet 'Mona'.

Dealers even offered package deals, whereby your scooter would be customised for you, including chrome paintwork, accessories and even increased power.

Dealers even offered package deals scooter would be customised for you paintwork, accessories and even incr

by your
...ding chrome
...l power.

The latter initially consisted of simply a larger barrel and piston and unreliable fuel injection. Some dealer Vespas were given 100 mph speedos to consolidate this increase, but in most cases only the speedo face was changed and the engine remained untouched. Thus was born the myth of the 80 mph Vespa SS 180.

If 1966 had been a good year for scooter sales, then 1967 was probably the worst. It was the dawning of the hippie era and demand for the bikes dropped off dramatically. Things got so bad, and dealers were faced with such a surplus of unwanted stock, that they turned to dramatic and sometimes outrageous measures in an attempt to out-do each other and grab the largest slice of a rapidly declining market.

For some reason the most outlandish creations were reserved for the Vespa SS 180. Motobaldet offered them up with a dummy petrol tank resting between the leg shields and Seat Supreme Motors turned out an amazing twin head lights version and naked women began to adorn their advertisements.

But it was left to Grimstead's to sink to an all-time low, with their summer of love, Psychedelic SS, which came in a Paisley paint finish, fairground motif (à la *Sgt Pepper*) or simple flower power stickers, all available from Hippy Eddy Grimstead. Cool, man.

Make your Vespa more attractive

handlebar mirror

fly screen

rear luggage rack

horn cover

rear crashbar and footrest

luggage rack

front crashbar

front bumper

with GENUINE VESPA ACCESSORIES

COMING AROUND AGAIN

By the end of the Seventies, scooter sales had plummeted to an all-time low. The old-style scooter clubs that had survived since the Fifties were still dotted around the north of England, but their numbers had dwindled dramatically.

Rallies were still held but attendance was poor, with most events attracting less than 100 riders and enthusiasts. The Northern Soul scene's scooter boys were also as scarce as the clubs that had spawned them and the new London Mod scene was a completely scooter-free affair.

The range of bikes available was also sparse, with Piaggio Vespa's output trimmed back from nine models in its heyday to a mere three — the Rally 200 and the small-framed 50 and 90 cc models. Marketing was cut to the bare minimum and dealerships closed down practically everywhere.

Lambretta had cut back even further than Vespa and for years only produced the GP 150 or 200, before completely closing down their factories in 1974 and selling the manufacturing plant machinery to India, where the GP continued to be produced. Lambretta turned their attention instead to building the Mini car for the Italian and French market, leaving the entire scooter industry virtually redundant for almost four years.

That was until 1980, when the unexpected happened — Vespa launched a brand new bike, the P range Vespa — a large-frame scooter available in 125, 150 and 200 cc versions. Vespa also made available a full range of accessories, from backrests, crash bars and flyscreens to carriers and mirrors.

The launch of the new P range coincided perfectly with the Mod revival, which was probably at its peak by 1981. That year's Brighton scooter rally attracted an estimated 8,000 scooters, made up of a mixture of modern and vintage bikes.

The old-style scooter clubs that had s around the north of England, but thei

ed since the Fifties were still dotted
bers had dwindled dramatically.

Unfortunately the scooter owners were also a bit of a mixture. Northern scooter boys, skinheads and Mods from London and the Home Counties were herded together by the over-anxious Brighton constabulary, thus causing more than a little friction and leading to the first reported violence involving Mods for 17 years.

The scooter was a popular mode of transport once again. Clubs began to reappear and rallies were well attended. The Vespa and Lambretta clubs of Great Britain started running separate and regular runs to seaside resorts, which in turn led to the formation of the 'pirate' runs organised by individuals who didn't want to be involved with segregated events.

Bob Morris: *"Those Lambretta and Vespa club events were a stupid idea because not everyone drove the same scooter. You'd have mates who had both, so if a group of say five out of seven of your mates had Vespas and two Lambrettas, two couldn't go. No-one wanted those sorts of restrictions."*

These new rallies were advertised as 'by Mods for Mods' and began to entice the real scooter enthusiasts who had bought old, original scooters and completely restored them to their own preferred, authentic style. This made scooter events all the more interesting and laid back because the old-style lights and mirror scooters wouldn't be out of place alongside a cut-down version, nor would a new P range rider be derided by an original GS owner.

Bob Morris: *"The thing about the P range... when it first came out in the early Eighties, they cost over five hundred quid, plus insurance. Back then loads of old scooters had been abandoned, you could pick them up for £50 off some old boy, and do them up.*

"I bought my first Series 2 TV off of a number plate dealer in Forest Gate for £90. It was hand-painted lime green with a big windscreen and a lunch box on the back. When I got it home I took the box off and scratched the paint off one of the side panels and it was chrome underneath. I got them both paint-stripped and did the whole thing up and went on the '81 rally. That bike would be worth £2,000 nowadays."

In 1994 Piaggio launched their 50th anniversary edition Vespa which was completely reshaped and restyled and broke with all tradition. A moulded fibreglass shell replaced the standard metal frame. It had an electric push button start and unremovable panels. It was originally meant as a strictly limited edition but Piaggio are still producing the scooter in vast quantities today, encouraged no doubt by the patronage of such high-profile riders as the Gallagher brothers, Damon Albarn and Chris Evans. Oh yes, there's also been a re-release of *Quadrophenia* on video with plans for a DVD version to follow later in 2000, proving that what goes around comes around and goes around again.

Scooter enthusiasts have always been well catered for magazine-wise, with publications like *Scooter* and *Three Wheeler* dating back to the late Fifties and not aimed at the youth market. Another publication appeared in 1979 entitled *Northern Mod Scene*, a small A5 glossy, published by Martin Dickson, and *Rallyist* by Nick Jolly. The year 1985 saw the first A4 glossy scooter magazine, *British Scooter Scene*, hit the shops and *Scootering International* joined the jostle for shelf space in 1990.

Both of these titles eventually merged into one under the heading *Scootering*, which has a distribution of over 130,000 readers to date. New contender *On Target*, first published in 1999, is now eager for a slice of the market.

TRANSMISION DIRECTA...

...la que parte del corazón. Vespa es el único scooter del mundo dotado de transmisión directa. Su motor transmite directamente toda su potencia a la rueda trasera. Es como un corazón poderoso y sano: sin cadenas, sin juntas, sin engranajes. Un poderoso corazón motorizado donde toda posibilidad de rotura o vibración queda eliminada. En todas partes del mundo, como un signo de nuestro tiempo, hombres y mujeres son felices con este scooter cordial.

Un año de garantía

Por otro lado, la scooter Vespa está prácticamente al alcance de todas. Estamos convencidos de que las facilidades de pago que concede Vespa encajan perfectamente en "su caso"

VESPA EL SCOOTER MAS VENDIDO DEL MUNDO

Vespa

...Y LA VIDA POR DELANTE

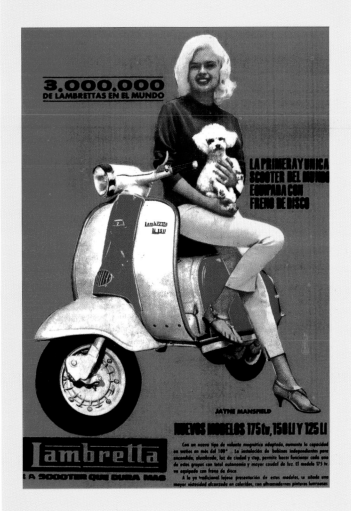

MANUFACTURERS OF VESPA SCOOTERS
SERVICE

SOMETHING'S MISSING
A new generation, a new direction?

The resurgence of the English Mod movement at the end of the Seventies gave rise to a completely different animal to the original Sixties version. In fact, it bore hardly any resemblance to it at all. It was nowhere near as stylish for a start, nor was it as complex or for that matter very popular. However, its devotees were every bit as obsessive, dedicated and, above all, as inventive and energetic as the original Modernists had been.

If the early Mods had found it hard to buy good, authentic items of American or French clothing, especially in a bleak postwar Sixties Britain, then trying to find anything decent at all in post-prog rock Seventies Britain was next to impossible.

Punk rock might have shaken up the country's music scene and industry, but it didn't do a hell of a lot to inspire sharp dressing. It's safe to say that in 1977, if you weren't sticking nappy pins or paper clips (yes, they did that) through your old school blazer, then you were strutting around town in a cheesecloth shirt, tank top and loons.

Feathercut hairdos were still in, big round-toed shoes were worn with glittery speckled socks and, if you were hip, Budgie jackets topped off the look.

Why the British birth rate didn't slump to an all-time low in the Seventies still puzzles many, but the bizarre truth was that something as simple as a button-down shirt was nowhere to be seen. There were no straight trousers or jeans in the shops, shoes with soles and heels under two inches high were available only to city workers or people in the legal profession and jackets with lapels that didn't act as an extra layer of shoulder padding simply didn't exist. So to be a Mod in the late Seventies proved to be something of a challenge.

The gateway to cool wasn't Carnaby Street any more. That particular thoroughfare was now a cheap and tacky tourist trap run by hippies. The clothes shops were long gone and the street's main attraction was now a drafty indoor market that sold unfeasibly amounts of Afghan coats and Coke bottles with fake polystyrene foam. Sartorial salvation could be sought only from second-hand clothes shops, army surplus stores or the reliable knitwear department of Marks & Spencer.

You had to dig deep. Sunday morning rites of passage meant a journey east to Brick Lane or Petticoat Lane, and a trawl through the dozens of tiny back street clothes shops and junk shops. These little shops had survived both the Great Fire of London and the Blitz, only to succumb to the nationwide epidemic of truly bad clothes that swept Britain in the Seventies. The shops looked and smelled condemned, the front windows were filthy and forever declaring a closing down sale and the owner always made you feel unwelcome but hidden away high on shelves and buried in back rooms were gems, gems I tells ya. Old stock, battered boxes of button-down shirts in perishing cellophane wrappers and covered in dust, windcheaters, crew necks and turtle necks. There wasn't much of it but it was there, dirty and forgotten and unwanted.

You could get an original US Army parka from the surplus shop at the Cheshire end of Brick Lane and sta-prest trousers from a stall next to the covered leather and sheepskin market at the Aldgate end of Petticoat Lane. Hidden away behind the rows of illegal pet stalls near the Commercial Road there was a shoe shop that sold corduroy lace-up shoes and pig-skin boots with elasticated sides, while a junk shop further down sold badges, military patches and even those little Esso man key rings and tiger tails. It was a far cry from the fashion-conscious West End but for the Seventies Mod that was about the extent of the choice.

Every now and then another little oasis of a shop would be found somewhere in London, a one-off discovery that might offer up a few decent shirts or a jacket, but this was rare and anyway the shop's location would never be revealed by whoever found it.

CARNABY CAVERN
MOD SUITS

IN STOCK
Mod Jackets £40. Available in Black, Grey,
Navy, Light Blue.
Mod Trousers £17.50. Available in Black,
Grey, Navy, Lt. Blue, Lirelle.
Button Down Shirts £9.95. In White, Lt
Blue, Navy, Black, Brown.
Mod Ties £2.95. Black, Grey, Navy.
Just in: 2 Tone Ties.
Jackets £40.00; Trousers (stock) £17.50;
Trousers Made To Measure £20.00.
Red/Blue and Blue/Tan.

MADE TO MEASURE
Jackets £40. For M.T.M. Please State
Chest, Height, Waist And Inside Leg
Measurement.
Trousers £20.

UNION JACKS
Jackets £85.00
Ties £4.50

MOHAIR SUITS
Jackets £50, Trousers £25. Available in
Black, Grey, Navy and Brown.
When Ordering Stock Items State Chest,
Waist and Inside Leg Measurements.
Deliveries on M.T.M. Items take 2 to 3
Weeks. Stock Items take 7 to 10 Days.
WE MAKE FOR: The Jam, Secret Affair,
Joe Jackson, The Specials, Back To Zero,
The Crooks and many more SO WHY
NOT YOU.
ALL PRICES INCLUDE POSTAGE AND
PACKAGE. CHEQUES & POs payable to
CARNABY CAVERN
3 NEWBURGH STREET LONDON
W1A 4GG. Tel 734 3971

"MOD" PARKA
GENUINE AMERICAN
FISHTAIL PARKA
AS WORN IN THE 60's
U.S. Army Surplus
Not new but in good condition
WITH FREE Can we Inners
ONLY £12.50 · 1.50 p.p
State chest size and height
SEND CHEQUES OR P.O.s TO:
PRINTOUT PROMOTIONS
28A ABINGTON SQUARE · NORTHAMPTON

There were still tailors in the West End, East End and the Old Kent Road willing to make a suit or jacket using original patterns but HP terms were a thing of the past and apprentice wages in 1977 and 1978 didn't quite stretch that far, so that was never really an option. But despite these setbacks it was just possible to put together a reasonably complete outfit. It may not have been new or made to measure, but it was inventive and it got you noticed... for all the wrong reasons. I've lost count of the amount of fights that dressing Mod got me into. Wearing a jacket, tie and an army parka could produce the most incredible rages in people, as inexplicable as they were unpredictable.

Some items of clothing became easier to find with the advent of power pop, which in this context describes the brief post-punk phase of groups that dressed with a distinct Sixties flavour. Bands like The Pleasers, Tonight, The Records and The Boyfriends all dressed with a Beatle-like uniformity and brought straight black suits, tab collar shirts and little knitted ties back into fashion. You still couldn't buy these things in the shops but we found out where these bands got them from, a little theatrical tailors just off Carnaby Street called The Carnaby Cavern.

The Carnaby Cavern wasn't so much a tailors as a stage clothes outfitter whose star customer outside of The Pleasers was Paul Weller. Back in 1977 and 1978, The Jam's spiky front man was the country's only high-profile Mod figurehead.

An inspirational character clearly in love with every facet of the original Mod movement, Weller wrote English pop songs in a similar (but angrier) vein to Ray Davies, trashed a Rickenbacker like Pete Townshend, and wore clobber you knew he hadn't traipsed around Brick Lane for. So for a short time the Carnaby Cavern became the place to go. The materials were usually of a dubious quality and the stitching was crap but it was affordable and, hey, Paul Weller went there and he looked good.

Steve McNerny was lead singer with The Pleasers: *"They used to put our pictures all over the front windows, us and The Jam, because that was the time, Record Mirror front covers and magazine pictures from Fab 208 and Jackie but inside it was really tacky. Inside it was all Roger de Coursey and Rod Hull, really bad outfits.*

"Me and the bass player, Bo, went there once to get something a little bit different to our normal three-button jobs and there were these two giant black blokes in there. They were about six foot four and they had these patterns all over the place of an outfit where the waistcoat was actually part of the trousers, all in one, and Bo said for a laugh, 'Let's get four of those done,' and I said, 'Fuck off, we'll look like the fucking Four Tops' and both of these giant guys turned round and said 'What's so bad about looking like us?' Paul was the only other musician I remember going there at the time, him and the others in The Jam, but after a while all these Mods went mad over it, all because of Weller. They actually made a Jam suit and advertised it in the NME quite early on."

and I said, 'Fuck off, we'll look like t giant guys turned round and said 'Wh

WESSEX HALL
Poole Art Centre

THE JAM
plus The Vapors

SUNDAY, 18th NOVEMBER 1979
7.30 p.m.
Admission £3.00

To be retained

RAINBOW 665
THEATRE 451

RAINBOW THEATRE
FINSBURY PARK 451

at 8 p.m.

M.C.P. presents
THE JAM plus Special Guests
at 8 p.m.

Sunday 16/11/80
Stalls

Sun NOVEMBER 16

Incl. VAT £4.00
T 39
TO BE GIVEN UP

STALLS

T 39 £4.00
Incl. VAT

For conditions of sale see over

cking Four Tops' and both of these
o bad about looking like us?'

PAUL

If you didn't belong to a tribe you were was violent and vicious...

ybody and it

History has painted Paul Weller as the Mod revivalist's sole inspiration and clothes-horse and to a certain extent this was true, but there were hundreds of other reasons why Mods reappeared on London streets at that particular time and it wasn't anything to do with the film *Quadrophenia,* which didn't hit British cinemas until 1979, at least a year on from the revival's first stirrings. So just what brought it about and who was responsible?

Buddy Ascott was a drummer from Bromley, South London, and would soon become one of the main players in the Mod revival as sticksman for The Chords: *"I don't know about other people but I'm sure everyone felt the same as me. I felt I was growing up in total isolation. I seemed to be the only person obsessed with The Who and the album* Quadrophenia *and this was 1974, '75. I was about 15 or 16 just as the punk thing was starting. I got into the album, I have to admit a friend lent it to me, and I played it, and to be honest I hated the music, I thought it was bloody awful. I got into it mainly because of the booklet. I loved the booklet it really appealed to me, the clothes, the haircut, and the girls who I thought were really horny and the violence — that's what really appealed to me. The whole thing appealed to me, it seemed like it was some sort of magical world we could never get back again and it was a world that I knew had existed because my brother was a Mod, but it just didn't seem to exist anymore. I liked the sharpness of the clothes. Well, they looked sharp to me because I was surrounded by a load of hippies in loon pants, so to me it was wonderful. I hated the contemporary music... I was only listening to the Stones, The Beatles and eventually the* Quadrophenia *album.*

"What we're forgetting, because we're looking at how Mods came back again in the Seventies, was that at the time tribalism was paramount. It was everything in the late Seventies and early Eighties. If you didn't belong to a tribe you weren't anybody and it was violent and vicious. There were still Teds on the Kings Road, punks, Mods, it mattered to people to belong and Mods came around purely by chance... the first time I saw a parka was (at) an Inmates gig at the Rock Garden and I saw this bloke down the front and I

nearly freaked. I was so taken aback, I pushed through and tapped him on the shoulder and said, 'Ere mate, where did you get your coat?' Imagine doing that now? And he said, 'Last Resort in Brick Lane run by a bloke named Mick.' We went down there the day after on the Sunday, four of us, and we all bought parkas. The three others with me didn't even know why they were buying them, they just thought they were cool-looking coats. Then we tried to get patches for them and I wrote to Shell Petrol to try and get the tiger tails and this was during the punk days. I was drumming in a punk band wearing a white boiler suit because Pete Townshend wore one."

Tony Lordan was another of the movement's front runners, equally isolated and way out west in Wembley: "It was punk that brought three-minute pop songs back into people's minds, going to clubs and seeing live bands, it brought back energy. Young people had energy and wanted to see groups and have a good time. Some people got tired of wearing scruffy clothes. Just like the original Mods didn't want to look like the beatniks, the Seventies Mods didn't want to look like punks, they wanted to look smart. A lot of the punk bands had Sixties influences, so it was inevitable that people would look back to the original Mods, which obviously The Jam had done and up to a point they did put it into people's minds, but I don't see how three blokes in mismatching black jackets and trousers could have headed a Mod revival. There were little pockets already around London.

"I was already into it. Obviously people might have taken some influence from Weller but you have to remember The Jam were not considered a Mod band at the time of the Mod revival. Paul Weller wasn't called a Mod. In a lot of ways he obviously was and he did it his own way. But no, The Jam didn't make the Mod revival any more than the Quadrophenia film did or Gary Bushell's interviews did. All they did was highlight something that was happening on its own."

So the tribe, small as it was, was growing and, strangely enough, it was growing in exactly the same way as it had done in the Sixties. Without any press or media coverage, it was created by individuals all drawing simultaneously from the same influences, all independently seeking out the same paradoxical identity, to be different yet part of the same.

Gary Crowley: "You would see someone in the West End and suspect that they might be into the same things and it was so unusual to see anyone that even looked remotely like a Mod that you would actually stop them and ask 'Are you a Mod, mate?'"

I was lucky. I had a friend from school called Martin Ward, who had followed me into Mod, so at least there were two of us. But that was rare. I swear if I ever saw another Mod they were always on their own, which brings me on to another important difference between the Seventies version of Mod and its Sixties counterpart: girls. There were no girls and I mean none whatsoever (well, there were one or two but they were few and far between). So what exactly did unite such a segregated bunch of loners at the end of the Seventies? The main ingredients so far had been the sounds of the Sixties, Quadrophenia (the album) and The Jam, whose importance, while undeniable, was not the catalyst for the revival to explode.

That would suggest we were all simply Jam fans, complete with matching 'fan-rabilia', a male version of The Bay City Rollers' tartan army (although I did have a scarf the same as Paul). No, we were Mods who liked The Jam.

The magazine that tells you what's on and where to go in London.
August 17-23 1979 No.487 35p

Time Out

Striking a familiar Chord.

This picture was taken last week, not in 1965. Inside Phil Shaw dusts off his parka, talks with The Chords and checks out the Mod Revival.

165

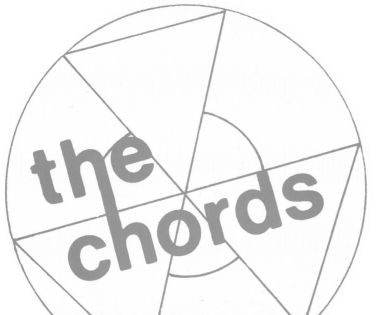

We still liked The Who, even though they bore no resemblance to the magical mental pictures we all carried around and, as for their contemporaries, they were either embarrassing (we had just witnessed the reformed Small Faces), dead or hopelessly deranged and lost in rock star indifference and indulgence (read Page, Beck, Clapton). So something was missing, something that every scene had except us — our own bands.

The fact was that in 1978, outside of seeing The Jam, there were no groups catering to us on the live music circuit. Power pop had been a Roman candle affair that had fizzled out just as quickly as it had arisen, thanks to

the arrival of an American band called The Knack in mid-1978. This barren live music landscape eventually saw yours truly reduced to going to see Smokie, because the lead singer had a Marriott centre parting, sounded like Rod Stewart and played a 12-string Rickenbacker.

This all changed one night in the Thomas A'Beckett when I met Billy Hassett. Billy was the singer-guitarist with a local Deptford band named The Chords and was in the pub trying to secure a gig for them. He had on a parka with the same army insignia that Chad wore in the *Quadrophenia* booklet, only upside down.

Pointing this out didn't seem to get us off on the wrong footing. In fact, we became firm friends, due to our mutual Modness, naturally. The Chords were your typical sixth-form school outfit, formed by Billy and his cousin Martin Mason (bass) along with school friends Paul Halpin (drums) and Chris Pope (guitar).

Billy Hassett: *"I was already a Mod, but there was no scene really to speak of. I don't think there was even 30 Mods spread out all over London. I got into it in much the same way all the new Mods did, loving the music of The Beatles and the Stones, at a time when it*

was all Roxy Music or Dark Side Of The Moon. *No-one was listening to that sort of music from the mid- to late Seventies. The whole Sixties thing wasn't acknowledged positively. The people like me who embraced it were, on the whole, out on a limb. The Beatles had only been broken up five years when punk happened and it became so unfashionable to like The Beatles.*

"*Some of the punk bands obviously took their influences from the Sixties bands, but they tried to hide it, or make out they were treating it with distaste. Gen X had target T-shirts all ripped up, the Pistols covered The Monkees and The Small Faces, but in their own style. I loved it when punk came along, I wanted to draw on that energy but I didn't identify with the image. I was watching every show that came from the Sixties, the* Man From U.N.C.L.E. *films were always on,* Secret Squirrel, The Monkees, Get Smart, *anything. I immersed myself, like we all did, in that imagery. Mod wasn't the pinpoint for us, it was the whole era and all we did was wrap it all up in one big coat, the parka. That was our statement. I mean I couldn't be a punk, I didn't want to destroy anything.*"

The Chords had been rehearsing together for almost a year, playing only to friends at parties or in local halls, crafting a stage act and set list that owed as much to punk rock as it did to the Sixties.

Brilliant and well-crafted originals like 'Something's Missing', 'Now It's Gone' and the era-defining 'Maybe Tomorrow' slotted in effortlessly alongside covers of The Small Faces' 'Hey Girl', The Action's 'I'll Keep Holding On' and The Beatles' 'She Said She Said'. All crashed out at breakneck speed, with a conviction and energy that I'd only seen in The Clash or, for that matter, in videos of the young Who. This was achieved in part by their recent new recruit drummer Buddy Ascott, whose drumming was as close to that of Keith Moon as it was possible to get.

Their first proper live gig was at the Kings Head pub in Deptford, on March 15, 1979, in front of perhaps a dozen Mods including Billy's brother Mike, an assortment of Millwall fans and a bar full of indifferent,

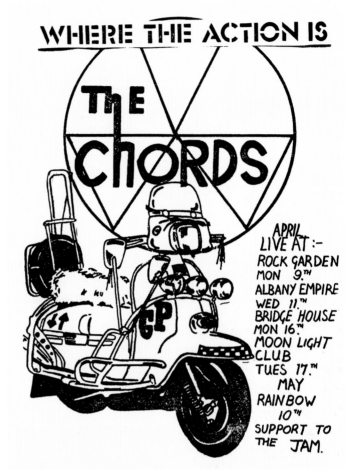

THE CHORDS ON TOP OF THE POPS, FEBRUARY 1980
(L-R: BUDDY ASCOTT, MARTIN MASON, BILLY HASSETT, CHRIS POPE).

THE PURPLE HEARTS AT THE LEGENDARY HOPE & ANCHOR.

local, drinkers. An inauspicious debut, but for the band a turning point. As for myself, I remember feeling an immense sense of pride in being part of this little clan of green-coated folk. It felt as though we had created our own little world. We now had a unique scene all of our own and it was all hidden away in deepest, darkest Deptford. No-one realised that across the Thames, in Canning Town, the same scene was being played out with another band called The Purple Hearts, an East End group unashamedly declaring themselves a Mod band, who had their own following and were already gigging.

Both bands had formed at roughly the same time, yet neither knew of the existence of the other. This was thanks to that good old-fashioned south and east London mutual distrust and dislike. The fact that The Chords supported Millwall and the Hearts West Ham may also have been a factor.

Billy Hassett: *"The first I knew of The Purple Hearts was a review in* Sounds *by Gary Bushell of a gig at the Bridge House, where they were called Mods. It was like, 'Hello, we better check this lot out.' It listed their next gig at The Moonlight Club in North London supporting The Damned. We thought, 'OK, North London! That's mutual ground, let's go up there and take some leaflets with us.' So me and Martin went up there with all these leaflets for The Chords and it was full of punks. The Purple Hearts had their little band of Mods but the place was rammed with punks, who didn't understand what we were all about, which was probably just as well. We watched the Hearts and they were great, we got to know their following and gave them our leaflets and as soon as The Damned came on, all the Mods went straight down the pub."*

The Purple Hearts were a completely different band to The Chords. They weren't as musically accomplished as their South London cousins, nor were their songs of the same calibre. But what they had over The Chords was their look. I'd never seen a band that looked as sharp as the Hearts. They had the whole Mod thing off to a T: East End arrogance, a moody-looking singer in Bob Manton and a flashy lead guitar player in Simon Stebbing. They were also all roughly the same height.

"It's a neat scene at the moment, but that's partly 'cos it's on a really small scale. Once it gets big you won't know where you are.
"At the moment most of the kids we know are mods. Like, if you see someone at a gig and they're a mod you'll go up and talk to them because of that.
"There's a type of comradeship like in the early days of punk."
Paul, 17, Swiss Cottage mod.

Mod is the sort of thing that should be accessible to everyone. Even the disco kids. The soul boys will be into it for the smooth image."
Bob, 18 Bethnal Green mod.

"I got into The Jam, I used to wear a suit when I first started going to see them and I just took it from there."
Gary, 17 Paddington mod.

"In the last few years, everything has come back — skins, teds, rockabilly — and the mod thing is the last to make a real comeback. So it's got to be the one with a real chance of staying."
Bob, 18, Bethnal Green mod.

"Most of the girls who go to the mod gigs with us wear pretty much the same clothes as the blokes. The main reason you don't see many girls dressed as mods is just that there's been no publicity about what they're supposed to wear.
"Unlike the blokes, they've had no-one to model themselves on. I suppose the only person in the last few years has been Faye Fife really . . . she dressed it although she never actually came out and said that she was a mod.
"Another thing is that most of the bands in London are too concerned with trying to look right as mods in terms of dress.
"Most of the best bands are from the suburbs — places like Enfield and Romford."
Tony, 19, Wembley mod.

Simon Stebbing: "We had the Mod look sorted even before punk. Me, Jeff and Bob definitely had the look, parkas and everything but we had racing bikes because we were too young to ride scooters. We all had the Quadrophenia album in school as opposed to Sweet Fanny Adams, we had Zombies records, Small Faces and Yardbirds stuff all on compilations because that stuff was really hard to get. It wasn't like now with box sets on everyone, back then compilations were a rare thing and ones with The Yardbirds or The Small Faces on were like... forget it."

Aside from Quadrophenia, the other big album that became a major contributing factor to the Mod revival was Bowie's Pin Ups, his cover album of songs by acts including The Pretty Things, The Mojos and, of course, The Who. We thought they were Bowie originals at first because of the credits on the back. They were all written in Bowie's handwriting and it was all jumbled up. All the information was there about his tribute to the Mod bands who played the Marquee or wherever, but unless you studied it, the whole thing looked like scribble.

Another thing that impressed me about the Hearts was their distinct pop art element. Their bass player, Jeff Shadbolt, whom Bushell had dubbed 'Just Jeff' ("I was being all arrogant in the interview when Bushell asked me my name and I said 'Jeff' and he said, 'Just Jeff?' 'Yeah, that's right mate, just Jeff' and he put it in the review"), wore black-and-white pop art patterns with bleached white hair. They also had a logo designed by Tony Lordan that was a nick from the Lambretta logo. It was the first time I'd seen a well-known brand name played around with in that fashion. Their following were all better dressed than The Chords' contingent too, very sharp and sussed. They had a swagger about them. Tony Lordan even had handmade jumpers in pop art patterns, big bold squares and stripes in all manner of colours.

Tony Lordan: "I first met the Hearts at a Boyfriends gig at the Nashville in 1978, December time. They were all there and they kept looking at us. I was there with my brother Mike and a guy called Bob Waterman, who was known in the Mod fraternity as Bethnal Bob. We were

THE PURPLE HEARTS (L-R: JUST JEFF, SIMON STEBBING, GARY SPARKS, BOB MANTON).

just sitting there and they kept coming past. We thought they were eyeing us up for a fight and we were working out our battle plan. Anyway, Simon and Jeff walked over eventually and said, 'You Mods?', 'Er yeah!' and Jeff said, 'We're Mods as well. We've got a gig next week', which was at the Hop Poles. It went from there.

"I first met The Chords at the Moonlight Club gig. They (The Purple Hearts) were supporting The Damned, who were going under the name 'The School Bullys'. Billy was down the front, I don't think he was too impressed. The way he described them (the Hearts) to me was that they were different to The Chords and that The Chords were heavier. But those two bands were the Mod revival. It was such a close thing, there wasn't anyone else worth a look in. There was another band, The Scooters from Enfield that were going around the time of the Hearts but they were absolutely awful and The Points who did a set of almost entirely Who and Jam covers and wore grey suits, but they had disappeared by 1979.

"I got a leaflet off of Billy Hassett advertising their next gig at the Kings Head. I remember it because Buddy, who I think had just joined, had all these little rows of arrows circling his drums and the pub had all these posters up calling it 'Modsville'. I went down there with Gary Crowley and Jeff and all these punks chased us down the road, pissed off that their pub had been taken over by Mods.

"Gary got whacked around the head with a studded belt and his ear was bleeding. It was like 'Quick get a milk bottle to throw.' I'd come all the way from Wembley to Deptford but that's how it was. Kids would travel right across London for a gig. Nowadays a band would have to do four gigs right around London because no one travels. It meant that much."

There's a certain trait in music that's almost uniquely British and it's known as the 'scene leader challenge', a situation in which two bands from one particular genre are set up as rivals. It's a time-honoured tradition that goes back to the original Beatles versus Stones title bout in the Sixties, Sweet and Slade in the Seventies, Spandau Ballet and Duran Duran in the Eighties, through to Blur and Oasis in the Nineties. The bands themselves would rarely participate in the farce, as on the whole they were all quite friendly with each other. But it filled the gossip columns and, most importantly, sold records.

The Chords and The Purple Hearts should have been prime candidates for this sort of shenanigans... but they weren't, because history was about to repeat itself and this new Mod scene was about to explode into the nation's consciousness, just as the original one had done in 1964. And when it did, both bands, their following and the originators and the earliest characters on the scene, would be overtaken and overshadowed — this time by an even tackier high street version of Mod than the one that had existed the first time round.

In late 1978 Pete Towshend was about to unleash his rock opera *Tommy* on a London stage for the first time at the Shaftesbury Theatre in Shaftesbury Avenue. A handful of us, including Billy Hassett, dressed as immaculately as possible, brazenly gatecrashed the première. Now I can only surmise that the bouncers at the theatre were old enough to recognise Mods when they saw them, and thankfully assumed we were meant to be there, particularly as a pissed Pete Townshend seemed delighted to see us.

Townshend, holding a bottle of vodka and swaying from side to side, told us of his imminent film project, a full-length feature based on the album *Quadrophenia* and how he was looking for a band to appear in it.

Simon Stebbing: "We saw an advert from The Who's management, looking for a band to appear in the film. They wanted tapes sent in. We knocked off a two-track demo in my garage but we didn't get the gig. We later found out The Chords had done the same, they didn't get it either. The Who wanted a retro-sounding band, which neither us or The Chords sounded like so we wouldn't have been right for it anyway. Some shithouse band from up north got it and who were they? To this day no-one knows who they were." (In fact, it was a group called The Sneakers.)

The Thomas A'Beckett became the regular haunt for the south London Mod collective and friends, in particular Tuesday nights, which was R&B night. Rhythm & blues was enjoying something of a renaissance in London in early 1979, thanks to bands such as Red Beans & Rice, The Little Roosters and The Inmates plus the higher profile Eddie & The Hot Rods and a bunch of burly bruisers from Southend called Dr. Feelgood.

Dr. Feelgood, led by singer and harp player Lee Brilleaux and his lunatic guitar-playing sidekick Wilko Johnson, had literally kicked open the pub doors for the R&B audience in England, who for a long time had been starved of any live action. Punk rock was no longer ruling the world and heavy rock was still a scorned dog gig-wise, so rhythm & blues looked set to clean up again. Only this time around it wasn't called R&B, it was dubbed 'Pub Rock' and it was pretty damn good. Weller may have been turning on a whole new generation to the genius that was The Who and The Kinks but bands like Feelgood were providing just as valuable a service for the music of Muddy Waters and B.B. King and, better still, you could cram up on it down the pub.

And there was no better place to sample pub rock than down the Old Kent Road. Once voted Britain's dirtiest street, the Old Kent Road was full from top to bottom with accommodating late night, live music at pubs such as The Apples and Pears, The Green Man and The Henry Cooper. It was a virtual netherworld of bands who for the most part were unconcerned about musical fame, fads or the West End club scene. Many of the musicians on the pub circuit had already known or been part of all three anyway and the ones who hadn't didn't seem to give commercial success a second thought.

The Old Kent Road had a music scene that survived all on its own, independent of the mainstream and trendier music clubs or venues. The resident band at the Beckett on a Tuesday night was Stan's Blues Band, a powerhouse outfit led by a guitarist called Dennis Greaves and the most formidable harp player I've ever seen, called Mark Feltham. (There was no-one named Stan in the band.) Their set list was an eye-opener too, the first time we'd heard the likes of Freddy King's 'Tore Down', Little Waters' 'Last Night' and Otis Rush's 'Homework'. We all thought Dennis must have been a lot older than us to have known such diamond tunes as these. In fact, he

turned out to be only in his early twenties, but his knowledge of the blues was incredible. He also had this ridiculously long guitar lead that enabled him to walk about the crowd while playing, which we were also impressed by. He could even walk out into the street with it. They eventually changed their name to Nine Below Zero and went on to forge a reputation as the hottest live band in Britain for a while, selling out the Hammersmith Odeon and demolishing Feelgood themselves on ITV's *South Bank Show*. They were also championed by none other than Alexis Korner who did several opening slots for the band and described them as the best outfit he'd seen since The Rolling Stones. Not surprisingly then, the Thomas A'Beckett was the 'in' place at that time, south of the river.

Dennis Greaves: *"I couldn't believe what was happening down that pub. We were playing all over south London and getting a bit of a following but nothing like the Beckett. It started off with just a couple of Mods and then a couple more until the scooters started lining up around the back. We were adopted by them, we weren't a Mod band as such, we were an R&B band... well, I suppose that made us a Mod band. Anyway, that was a very special time and later when we became Nine Below Zero, a lot of that Mod thing came with us, all over the country."*

Oh yes, scooters. Another glaring difference between the revival and the original movement. The original Mods, on the whole, all owned scooters. Not so in 1979; well, not at first. The scooter was as hard to find as the clothes and anyone who had one was the envy of one and all. The first time someone turned up on a scooter, the entire pub emptied en masse to see it. Elvis could have walked by unnoticed, such was the excitement that this chariot of the gods caused. It was owned by a bloke named Mick who had lived up north where such machines were rumoured to be widespread. It was a Lambretta TV 200, with the complete works: lights, mirrors and crash bars, which he said he'd invented and patented. And in our naivety, we all believed him.

I eventually tracked down a scooter of my own, thanks to an old school friend, who told me that his neighbour was, astonishingly enough, giving one away. A cream and green TV 200, which I was legally too young to drive. An immaterial problem as it turned out because the thing hardly ever went anyway, but a friend swapped the badges over to limit the risk, just in case.

There was a railway bridge between my flat and the Thomas A'Beckett that I tried to span on three separate occasions. The scooter expired each time at the summit, leaving me no choice but to embarrassingly coast down the other side and up to the pub doors. I now knew why my friend's neighbour wanted shot of it — it was useless. I eventually got so fed up with pushing it along that I parked it up at the end of a line of motorbikes and mopeds that were for sale outside what used to be Scoot-a-long, and abandoned it, Paddington Bear style. I made do with riding on the back of another mate's bike after that, a bloke called Don, who'd arranged for The Chords to play their first away gig, on March 17, 1979, at a railway pub called the Wellington, opposite Waterloo main line station.

Billy Hassett: *"It was one of those typical dirty, smelly, commuter pubs that people only use while waiting for their trains during the week. The guvnor agreed to us playing there because the place was empty on weekends and he was desperate for any trade. There was a rehearsal studio right around the corner, called Alsaka, which was run by one of The Boyfriends, Pat Collier, and we booked in there a couple of days beforehand to rehearse and the guvnor came in to hear us and told us 'Yeah, you can do this, Saturday, but you can't charge to get in and I'm not paying yer.'"*

The excitement leading up to that gig was unbelievable, I drew up a flyer that triumphantly announced to the country that the Mod movement was firmly on the move, even if it was only going across South London, about four miles. A couple of us went in to the West End and stuck them up in every sympathetic record shop we could find, from Rock On record shack in Soho market to Tumbleweed Connection behind Selfridges. When the night came, our entire entourage prepared to move out, three scooters and the rest on the number 1 bus. We were met by around 200 drunken Southampton

supporters who were quite happily ensconced in both bars and seemed in no hurry to return home. It looked bad but despite losing count of how many times I answered "No" to the slurred inquiry "Oi, are you lot squaddies", it went off without a hitch. The band had proved they could hold it together and deliver the goods regardless of an audience's initial indifference. It was a breakthrough quality that would make them very popular with crowds outside the Mod movement throughout their career. Unfortunately it would also highlight the unfair criticism that would later befall them when the Mod label turned into a claustrophobic pigeon-hole that would eventually destroy both The Chords and the Purple Hearts.

The Wellington, on the other hand, did very well out of it all. Following The Chords' successful debut, the chuffed landlord had predictably offered them every Saturday night — without pay, of course. It was the beginning of a residency that would prove within a matter of weeks that the movement was on the increase, and moving more quickly than anyone had thought. The Wellington became the single most important venue in the development of the scene. Its central location and handy rail links made it possible for everyone to get to, plus it was free. The landlord confided in me after only a couple of weeks that the Saturday night session made more money than the rest of the week's sessions put together.

PAUL WELLER DROPS IN UNNOTICED AT THE CHORDS GIG AT THE WELLINGTON, 1979.

Billy Hassett: *"The speed and the gravity at which it was all happening was frightening. No-one had any idea why this was getting so big so soon. We had come from a lowly little band who played for our friends, to suddenly pulling in a couple of hundred people all within two to three months."* Indeed, as early as the band's third appearance the word had spread to the mighty *NME* who dispatched scribes to investigate. Polydor and EMI A & R men actually turned up, and on a weekend night too. Even Paul Weller's curiosity had finally got the better of him and he and his girlfriend Gill turned up one night to see what all the fuss was about.

I'd known Paul casually on and off for a little while, having first recognised him as a kid from a caravan site in a place called Selsey Bill in Sussex. I was down there serving one of my yearly six-week sentences, which my parents cheerfully referred to as my summer holidays. This meant me and my brother Mick being packed off for a month and a half to a caravan on a site called Green Lawns, to be looked after by our nans, Ivy and Alice. Paul stayed with his family on a site nearby called West Sands and I clearly remember seeing him at the site's club house, called The Embassy, although I didn't really talk to him until the early Jam gigs at the 100 Club in 1977. I would also bump into Paul simply walking around the West End, which both he and I seemed to

spend a lot of time doing. It was on one of these chance encounters that I told him about The Chords and the whole Wellington happenings. I needn't have bothered as it transpired because his hairdresser, the village barber, was in the same street as the record shop Tumbleweed Connection. This was a regular fly-posting stop off point for us and little A4 flyers depicting a scooter emblazoned with arrows and announcing The Chords, hadn't failed to catch his eye.

Less than five weeks later, on May 11, 1979, The Chords were supporting The Jam at a sold-out Rainbow Theatre and over half the audience were Mods. Both The Chords and the Purple Hearts both had record deals: The Chords were on the Jimmy Pursey-run Polydor subsidiary JP Records and The Hearts were on Fiction. Both bands and their following had been the subject of Janet Street Porter's *London Weekend* show and both bands were about to release their debut singles.

Gary Sparks: *"I thought, 'This is brilliant, something huge is going to happen now.' We had the world within our grasp. The Chords sounded completely different to us but we were all the same in spirit, so we weren't about to step on each other's toes. We knew there would be other bands following on, but this was our moment."*

THE PURPLE HEARTS AT THE BRIDGE HOUSE, CANNING TOWN.

AN INTERVIEW WITH GARY CROWLEY

"When I was a kid it was all Gary Glitter. I don't know how I discovered The Beatles, I can't remember being aware of The Beatles when they were happening. It might have been a documentary on TV or something like that. I can't remember whatever started it but when it did I was totally enamoured by them to the point of selling everything else that I had. I had to have every Beatles record and every Beatles book. I would have been 11 or 12, something like that, in about 1974/75. I got totally immersed in The Beatles and through them I discovered the Sixties and after that every school project I did had a Sixties theme, or a Beatles theme, which led to the Stones and then The Who and then bang, punk happened.

"I was old enough by then to be aware of that but I wasn't really into it. I was still wrapped up in my Sixties world, until I saw pictures of The Jam in 1976. I read some interviews and though 'Wow! This is the band I've been waiting for, the singer's only a few years older than me, 17 or 18 years old.' The suits, the ties, the Motown thing, they were the fucking band, from The Beatles straight to The Jam.

"We turned our school magazine into a fanzine and somehow rang up Paul Weller's house one day and his sister answered and she said, 'Well, he's here — you can speak to him' and he said, 'Why don't you come and see me?' I was 15 at the time and in a phone box outside our school. At lunch-time we used to ring up record companies and blag records and tickets for gigs. So I met him the next day and after that I knew what direction I was going in.

"I had other references to draw on too. My uncle, for example, had been a Mod and when I was into the whole Sixties thing before punk had come along, he used to come over to our flat once a month. He grew up just off the Edgware Road and there was a famous youth club there called The Four Feathers, which was a real Mod club. He had a scooter and had gone to the Brighton and Hastings punch-ups and he used to tell me all these great stories.

"But after *This Is The Modern World* came out, all my friends on the estate were into punk and a couple were into Siouxsie & The Banshees and I was into The Jam and

GARY CROWLEY (RIGHT) SWINGING WITH THE AUTHOR, GOLDEN SQUARE, LONDON, 1979.

Fame and fortune for Deptford mods **the Chords** seems imminent with the strong possibility of the boys signing to **J. Pursey's** label, and a gig lined up at the Rainbow supporting the **Jam** on May 10.

Paul Weller clocked them at the Wellington in Waterloo and obviously mucho impressed, arranged the support forthwith.

The Chords
Kings Arms

AWLREADY AWLREADY, the letter we printed recently from the Romford punks was probably the most sensible statement to-date about the rapidly sprouting Mod Renewal. It's happening, right, but it's happening in *fun*, it's a laugh, and everyone knows it'll all get gumbyised when 'Quadraphenia' comes out and the Biz and *The Sun* catch on anyway.

So what us rock journalists are after are the groups who aren't just after riding 10 day media miracles, the ones with the musical muscle to ensure survival when the fad fades into Anne Murray mania or whatever else catches idle paper appreciation.

Groups like The Chords. I'm here tonight on a tip-off from one of Southend's leading mods who whispered hot nothings into me shell-likes to the effect that The Chords were 'better than the Purple Hearts', and with all due respect to that rapidly developing Romford combo, he wus right, (and I ain't just saying that cos they come from South East London either).

The Chords are Bert Scott (drums), Billy H (vocals/rhythm guitar), Chris Pope (lead guitar) and Martin Mason (bass/vocals); a powered piece who've been together since March '77 when they started out on Tamla standards, and who've matured through line-up changes into a surprisingly tight and competent modern Mod music machine, their own songs rubbing shoulders with choice golden oldies in a 13 song set.

Can't tell you much about presentation as the band were hid from sight behind a sea of parka-packing modsters but the sound was well impressive — despite a dodgy vocals-too-low sound mix — combining crashing power chord drive in a Jolt/Jam vein with a convincing grasp of melody. Pop with guts ma babes, and well structured stuff to boot.

Of their own songs 'Something Missing', 'Maybe Tomorrow' and 'I Don't Wanna Know' made the strongest impact on first hearing but the real test came with the covers — 'Knock On Wood', 'She Said', 'Tell Me,' and 'Circles' — which they handled with admirable aplomb; a full-driving encore version of the Small Faces 'Hey Girl' being particularly excellent.

What's left to be said? I'm not gonna jump on any bandwagons and sprout lengthy after-dinner speeches about the Mod Movement. No, what's important is ... well as/despite the trapp- ... ... a fine pro-

I FOLLOWED The Word anmd headed briskly for The Cambridge Hotel, a sprawling suburban affair in London's northern borders. The Word: a revival? Well, the parka-clad youths and Simon Templar besuited mod-types were in little doubt. This was the post-punk saviour! Lager glasses were clutched nervously, hasty glances were exchanged between strangers, assessing coolness, the clique complete.

All very well, but where's the proof? Hyping the silly seeds of fashion, fads or (even) musical renaissances is a terrible business and I'm pleased to have been associated with *Snouds* relative sang froid in the face of fizzy press hysteria.

The whole instant 'new wave' stench of the phenomenon admittedly gave me a less than optimistic attitude towards the gig from the start. But inside, the definite buzz of something clear and alive gave me hope for something beyond mere business yik-yak. It was so nice to see so many young people who were *obsessed* by somebody as significant as The Jam.

First band on were Back To Zero, who were, it appeared, the goods. Gawks, bizarrely obsolete youths trying out their shiny new shoes and shiny new suits, leaving the audience slightly bemused by their authenticity somehow. The sound was powerful and strongly spiced by the bespectacled guitarist's trusty, erratic rickenbacker, the set ending in a Who-like blaze of screeching feedback. Yeah, Back To Zero I found highly recommendable as a mod-revivalist unit, treading along (coming back to them again) The Jam's excellent course, but failing to go beyond that point of influence.

But The Purple Hearts? I couldn't understand their outward allegiency to, uh, mod (presumably, the term), coming across behind the slightly sickly veneer of 'unimod' (nice clothes, nice faces, nice pose) as a late '79 punk band, yaarghing cocky Cockney all-boys-together voices, Deep Purpley guitars, a conscience, *et al.* The Rickenbackers seemed all too compulsory more than indispensible.

The songs were at best promising, but compared to the few genuine young hopefuls (yer Protexes, Undertones . . . uh, nobody else) they don't stand-up. The songs, 'Jimmy' can be taken as an example, were concentrated around uninspired powerchords, lacking style and (so surprising) real identity. The Purple Hearts were not impressive.

The Chords similarly failed to catch the imagination. Again a focal-point lead singer yowled public grievances over a less than confident backing, the band failing to move, leap, remotely excited. Maybe they lack assurity on stage (a major problem), maybe they've got their eyes set glassily upon some distant, mercenary 'new thing' mirage (unforgiveable), one can't be certain on the evidence of one gig.

The major problem was the trio of bands' simple dearth of attack, which is something I was genuinely surprised not to find: the ordinariness was overwhelming. Indeed, I was prompted through sheer boredom to traipse wearily into the adjoining inn, precluding The Chords' set. I was interested to discover that a fair number of mod punters had taken the same few steps to a pint and the sound of 'Strange Town' on the droning duke-box. Yeah, I think the kids *do* understand after all.

DAVE McCULLOUGH

The suits, the ties,
they were the fuck

otown thing,
nd, from The Beatles straight to The Jam.

The Clash, everyone had their favourites. But just as that came out I left school and went to work at Decca Records as an office boy, which was the best job you could have had really because even though they had nobody signed to the label apart from the Smurfs and Isla St. Clair or Glenda Jackson's spoken-word album, they had The Small Faces' back catalogue, London Records and the early Stones. There was a great treasure trove of stuff to look through. Also, it was in the West End, in Marlborough Street and from here you would bump into people like yourself and Tony Lordan, who went on to be in Department S.

"We used to get every music paper and magazine going from the paper stall opposite Liberty's, and that's how I read about The Purple Hearts playing at the Middlesex Hospital, which is on Cleaveland Street, and I remember going to that and Tony Lordan was there and Grant Fleming and another bloke who worked for Sham 69 who everyone called Woody Allen. It was all word of mouth and I imagine it was exactly like that the first time around. People swapped phone numbers because we all shared something. Everyone gravitating towards the same gigs until you became a crowd, it just snowballed. The Wellington pushed it even further. The Bridge House was another one, but that was a bit far out. The Wellington had the big Saturday Night thing going on and it was great, you sort of had this instant group of mates and this lasted for a short time really, maybe a year or two and then it was gone. I got offered Danny Baker's old job at the *NME* and you replaced me at Decca and it sort of petered out soon after.

"Skinheads started appearing everywhere and there started to be trouble at a lot of gigs. But you still went — you had to go — it was important to go. I wouldn't go to half those gigs now if you paid me a thousand pounds."

EDDY PILLER WAS CO-FOUNDER OF EIGHTIES MOD RECORD LABEL COUNTDOWN AND LATER ACID JAZZ

I can remember the day my life changed. I was on the tube at Camden Town station on the way home from a Stiff Little Fingers gig. It was February 1979. I was 15 and up until that point I had been bumping along between The Buzzcocks and The Damned, picking up as many punk singles as my Saturday job in Mister Byrite would allow. My one ritual observance was a regular trip to Small Wonder Records by bus to Walthamstow where Hippy Pete introduced me to the exciting world of underground youth culture. But try as I might, I could never really be a punk. I was profoundly affected by it (especially the music) but I wasn't actually a part of it. Nihilism just wasn't my bag.

So, there I was with my friend Tris on the Northern Line. We were in a carriage packed with sweaty Stiff Little Fingers punters and I was writing 'West Ham United' on the carriage door. Suddenly, the bloke behind me tapped me on the shoulder and asked to borrow my marker. He was tall with spiky hair, wearing a target T-shirt and a weird iridescent three-buttoned jacket. He looked cool but different. There was something that set him apart from the other passengers, but at that stage I hadn't realized what it was. He took the pen and wrote the legend 'Mods' just below where I'd written 'West Ham'. There was an arrow on the top of the 'D'.

When he handed the pen back we asked him what he'd meant. I mean, Tris and I both knew what Mods were, but neither of us had ever met one. In fact neither of us could even conceive of one at that time. He told us about a couple of bands that him and his mates followed around. He assured us that if we liked Stiff Little Fingers, we'd love them too. He also told us to meet him that Saturday afternoon at the back of The West Side, Upton Park.

When Saturday came we took the bus up to the Army and Navy in Manor Park. I brought some desert boots and a US parka and was wearing an old button-down

shirt of my dad's. We had 'turned' Mod... At the match there must have been a hundred or so Mods interspersed with at least a thousand crop-headed skins in Harringtons or Donkey jackets (there were even a few in butcher's aprons). There was no real animosity between the two groups at that stage. Probably because the Mods were novel and so few.

EDDIE PILLER FAR RIGHT.

I finally realized what it was I had liked about the Mod on the tube. It was his arrogance. His understanding that, from his own perspective, he was different to everybody else... He and his friends had deliberately embraced a culture and a set of codes that set them apart from their contemporaries. The promised gig came around a week later and the band were called The Chords. It was only their second gig, at a pub called The Green Man in Plumstead. The journey meant five buses and the Woolwich ferry. If we were apprehensive, there was no need. The doors swung open to reveal about 75 people dressed in a cross-section of what passed for Mod fashion in early '79. The atmosphere was relaxed and the spirit of camaraderie was strong. It is hard to explain if you weren't there at the time, but it was like we were standing at the threshold of some great adventure.

Within weeks we were regulars at The Bridgehouse in Canning Town. This was famous in the East End for being a hard skinhead pub. It was run by a famous East End boxing family called The Murphys (son of the guvnor was Glen Murphy, the *London's Burning* star) who were involved in the scene from the early days. Secret Affair played first and pulled 400 people

It was like we were standing at the threshold of some great adventure.

THE BRIDGE HOUSE
23 BARKING ROAD, CANNING TOWN. E16

Monday, April 16th   50p
Mod's Monday with
SECRET AFFAIR
+ The Chords

Monday April 30th   50p
Mods Monday with
SECRET AFFAIR
+ Les Elite

Monday May 7th   50p
Live Recording of Mods
Album on Bridge House Records
SECRET AFFAIR
+ The Mods

Monday May 14th   50p
Mods Monday with
THE CHORDS
+ The Scooters

Thursday May 24th   40p
LITTLE ROOSTERS
+ BEGGAR

Monday May 28th   50p
Mods. Monday with
SECRET AFFAIR
+ The Mods

They weren't slow to see the commercial potential of a regular night and the 'Mod Mondays' became the focal point of the scene in East London, spawning the live showcase *Mod's Mayday* album and releasing it on their own label (the first 500 were emblazoned with the famous '15 new nunbers' spelling mistake on the front cover, producing the Mod revival scene's first rare record). Every Monday bands like The Mods, Scooters, Beggar, Secret Affair, Back To Zero, The Teenbeats and The Purple Hearts would play and you would meet   up with fresh crews from all over the country who'd made the trip. A scene was starting

to develop. You'd meet up with the same faces at the weirdest of places. Grant Fleming, Goffa Glading and The Maximum Speed crew, Tony Lordan and Vaughan Toulouse from *Get Up and Go* fanzine, (they were always plugging their own band, Guns For Hire, who went on to have a Top 30 hit with *Is Vic There?*, under the new name of Department S). Gary Crowley, Hoxton Tom, The Wembley Girls, The Boreham Wood and Bethnal Green crews were some of the early participants.

The Bridgehouse was by no means the only Mod venue. There was also The Wellington in South London and The Global Village in Charing Cross. But by far the most important venue to the Mods was The Marquee. Steeped in an impressive Mod history since the Sixties, the club led the way in the West End. All went well till the summer when The Jam's secret John's Boys date, quickly followed by a Secret Affair headline during which Ian Page distributed 200 'glory pills' to the audience (yes, they were real blues, I know because I snaffled a few of them...), resulted in a Mod ban at the Marquee. As well as running Mod gigs, it was the first place I heard a DJ playing Sixties soul. His name was Jerry Floyd, he was an old guy who was part of the furniture there. He used to deejay every night, mainly with rock bands. It wasn't until the Mod bands started playing there that he really came into his own. I think he used to be a Mod in the Sixties and when he started playing those original US soul sevens he introduced me to a whole new parallel Mod universe.

Fanzines were really important too. After *Quadrophenia* there were literally thousands of them. *Maximum Speed, Direction, Reaction, Creation* and *Roadrunner* were probably the most influential in '79 and early '80, but after that the next generation came forward to carry the banner. Most of the earliest faces had been completely disillusioned by the media coverage and the new generation of Mod recruits drawn in by the hype and had gradually drifted away.

By the middle of 1980, most of the main bands were feeling the media backlash pressure. Clothes and scooters gradually became more important and fashions within the scene were changing. The first real shift was, ironically, towards the psychedelic influence of '67. By late summer the Paisley shirt was de rigueure, and the double-breasted Regency jacket had made an entrance. Paul Weller wasn't alone in looking at the later swinging Sixties scene as the natural Mod progression. Brian Betterage, the diminutive but stylish lead singer of Back To Zero was dabbling and the Purple Hearts, who had always looked to Sixties garage punk as an influence, were starting to perform numbers like *'Let's Get A Burger, Man'* and *'Hazy Darkness On A Sunny Day'*... We used to frantically search around for Paisley in the remaining gentleman's outfitters in the East End.

PRE-CHARLATAN MARTIN BLUNT'S EMPTY GLASS IS CONSPICUOUSLY IGNORED BY DJ BOB MORRIS.

Places like Davis in Stepney Green and Stevie Starr in East Ham provided original Denson shoes, and once you got to know the guvnor (which for some reason in those crusty old East End shops took time) you'd finally be invited 'round the back' to check their original Sixties remnants. Many a herringbone double-breasted, high-collared jacket saw the light for the first time since it had been made in '66, and the prices were of course a tenth of what it would cost to have had it made. It was much the same for scooters. I bought my first (a Vespa 90) from a group of older Mods in Preston Road, up near Wembley. I didn't know anything about scooters at the time, but I thought £25 was a bargain... The real problem I faced was getting it back to Woodford. I'd never driven a bike before. Didn't know about gears, MOTs, insurance or vaguely how to ride it. I was 15. I wheeled it down to the Metropolitan line station, down the steps and waited till the train pulled in. The guard went ballistic and refused to let me wheel this (rather knackered looking) contraption into a carriage, but eventually relented when I pointed to the 30-plus stairs I'd wheeled it down and told him that I could never get it back up... The real problem came when I was trying to change for the Central Line at Liverpool Street. The bastard put itself into gear as I was rolling it down some steps and roared off along the platform with a life of its own. I didn't have a fucking clue how to stop it (I didn't even know where the gears were) and it came to rest crashing into one of those old wooden benches on the platform, scaring the shit out of just about everyone. Eventually the train pulled in to Woodford and I was safe (apart from the inspector at the gate, who told me that taking motor scooters on the tube was illegal and I'd have to take it back to where I'd got on, especially as I'd only bought it a child ticket'.

Scooters started becoming more important. In '79, bank holidays were only really an event on the Monday itself, with people getting the train down to Southend or Clacton for the day. By late '80, scooters made it much easier to set off on the Friday night to make a whole weekend of it. The run was born. For a while there was no real organisation, and groups of friends just made the trip to one of the traditional venues (usually Brighton or Margate), but by '81 there seemed to be an overall consensus as to where people would go... A typical 1981 run was to Brighton, and for our crowd began at the main pub in the area, The Castle on Woodford High Rd. All the Woodford would meet at about eleven o'clock on the Saturday morning. There'd be maybe a dozen scooters and a couple of cars. Over the next couple of hours the local crews would pull into the car park. Maybe ten would roll in from Wanstead, led by Steve Jarvis who was definitely one of the local faces, 30 scooters from Hainault (which was an important crew, because that's where all the speed

MORE TV HIGHLIGHTS
COURTESY OF DANNY BAKER.

CHAD FREDERICKS AT ARABELLA'S, 1981.

came from), one by one Chingford, Walthamstow, Epping, Loughton and even crews from Waltham Abbey and Cheshunt would pull up, to ever increasing cheers, until the car park was full to bursting with a sea of green-clad, scooter-revving Mods. When the pub kicked us out at two o'clock a hundred odd scooters, 15 cars and a couple of vans snaked their way through the East End, rendezvousing with other groups of scooters, until we reached the old Westminster Tea bar opposite the Houses Of Parliament. This was probably the main meeting place for all London Mods at the time and on any given night of the week you could guarantee at least a dozen scooters getting their late night cup of tea (in those days there were very few late licensed clubs, and most Mod do's were held in South London pubs). Anyhow, by mid-afternoon there must've been a thousand or so scooters milling around Parliament Square and the snake gradually wound its way down the Embankment and over Vauxhall Bridge, always travelling at the lowest common speed (that of a Vespa 50 special), 35 miles an hour. It's impossible to explain the extraordinary feeling that riding with a thousand other scooters gives you. It didn't really happen that often (many times a couple of hundred, but big, big groups like this were rare). At each main junction more and more scooters joined the swell. Ilford, Rainham, The Fulham Wasps, The Nomads, The Paddington, Hornchurch, Luton. Wave after wave. Normal hostilities were suspended for the weekend (for example the East London Mods and The Paddington were always fighting around this time) and as we drove through Brixton we cheered the rioters smashing the streets up. They even suspended action for 15 minutes as we drove through, and we felt a definite solidarity with the anti-establishment rioters, whose enemy was the same as ours (the police). They cheered, we cheered and then we were into Streatham.

When our convoy rolled into town on Saturday evening we met with police roadblocks at every entrance. Virtually everyone was searched for drugs and weapons and hundreds were actually turned back to try again further down the coast in Hove or Rottingdean and work their way into town by different routes. Those without a B&B were shepherded up to the golf course on the coast where tents were pitched and people started meeting up with stragglers. Tony Class put on a do, (at the Drill Hall, I think) that evening , and although tickets were like the proverbial gold dust we all managed to blag our way in, only to walk into one of the largest free-for-all Wild West fights I have ever seen. Literally hundreds a side. No one really seemed to know who'd started it or, even worse, who was fighting against whom, but it went off no mistake and the police cleared the venue by ten. Five hundred pumped-up lunatics found themselves herded down towards the seafront where they could be properly supervised. When the latecomers arrived there was already a riot in progress. It had started at about seven o'clock when some Mods had decided to ride the ornamental train that ordinarily plied its trade taking old ladies from the pier to the other end of the promenade. By the time a hundred or so Mods had crammed their way on, the police turned off the electricity, and announced by megaphone that anyone not leaving the train would be physically removed and arrested. Well, wave a red rag at a bull, why don't you. Everyone piled off the train and pushed it along for a couple of hundred yards until it

came off the rails and fell over. The police baton-charged, but nobody ran away. It was like everyone had been affected by the general feeling of rebellion sweeping through the country, and so ably demonstrated by the scenes as we drove through Brixton on the A23. The Mods countercharged and the police gave ground. After an hour of sporadic baton charges countered by bottle – and deckchair – throwing youth, the police withdrew to the top of the embankment and the mob of (by now 2,500) Mods had control of the seafront esplanade. A tea-hut got petrol-bombed, cars were overturned and snatch squads were doing their best to seize the leaders... I'd never experienced anything vaguely like this before, and the police just didn't know how to respond. The elements came to their aid when it started to rain. Gradually groups drifted off to tents or B&Bs, and eventually, when the numbers milling around were much reduced, the police moved in to take control of the area. The Mods who hadn't managed to get out of the ringed control area were all searched, and had their shoes removed and dumped in a pile on the beach. At four in the morning, the police told the thousand-odd (shoeless) Mods to collect their shoes and were escorted to the town gates on the A23, and told never to come back to Brighton.

The scene the next morning was one of abject chaos, but the papers were full of Brixton and the hundred or so Mod arrests hardly warranted a mention. In fact, it seemed like half of the country had rioted over that weekend, so maybe an explosion between Mods and the police had been inevitable... Most bank holidays weren't as event-filled as this one, but there were plenty of amazing journeys to a variety of venues from Rhyl to Lowestoft and from Weston-Super-Mare to the Isle of Wight.

Gradually, the Mods of the late Seventies and early Eighties just faded away. By '83, Northern Soul was the staple diet of all the Mod clubs, and the good nights were becoming few and further between. *Extraordinary Sensations,* the last of the original '79 fanzines packed up in early '85, and most of the older Mods on the London scene were searching for pastures new.

We found them in the embryonic jazz scene based around the DJs Gilles Peterson and Paul Murphy. These two ran a couple of jazz dance sessions at the Electric Ballroom in Camden Town and the Wag in Wardour Street, and to their amazement the disillusioned stylists found both the music (the likes of *Wack Wack* by the Young Holt Trio, Jimmy Smith and Jack McDuff were getting hammered) and the style of the scene itself refreshing. Nineteen eighty-six was the important year. By then most of the London-based youth cultures that were into black music were on their last legs. Not just the Mods, and the Northern Soul scene, but also the Casuals with their jazz funk and Italian sportswear. Rare Groove, with its attention to the smarter styles of the Seventies, was over too and the reign of the skinhead finally became merely a memory. In short there were a lot of people into soul, jazz and funk, who weren't being catered for, and almost naturally they all seemed to mix themselves together around the burgeoning jazz scene. The fashions were broadly Mod, but without any of the blinkered, small-minded attitudes that accompanied the Mod scene in '86. The scene grew, eventually being called the Acid Jazz scene by the media and Mods could quite easily co-exist within it. As the scene progressed, so the music became even more accessible to someone brought up on the Mod philosophy. Even the bands had a familiar ring to them. The James Taylor Quartet, with the two Mod Taylor brothers, the deliciously kitsch Corduroy, and the Small Faces-influenced Mother Earth. The difference between these bands and the majority of the Mod bands that had gone before, was the fact that these weren't Mod bands, they were bands that had Mods in them. The media's long-standing hatred of all things Mod didn't have an effect, firstly because they hadn't really spotted the link between the two, and secondly because long-standing Mods like Paul Moody and John Harris had risen to the editorships (or features editorships) of magazines like *Select* and *NME.* Things were gradually swinging back in Mod's favour. People around the world did notice the philosophical link between the two, and promotors Frederic Ekander in Sweden, Leif Nueske and Henry Storch in Germany, all long-standing Mods, used the underground networks they'd set up on the Mod scene to promote the latest incarnation of Mod, the

Acid Jazz scene. Paul Weller was heavily involved in the scene, vocalling tracks with Mother Earth and working with long-time Reading Modernist and Young Disciple, Marco Nelson. For four long years, the world was letting the Mods back in through the back door, clearing the decks of political baggage, and setting the scene for the next popular explosion of Modernism that accompanied Oasis, Blur and The Ocean Colour Scene.

ACID JAZZ MODS, CORDUROY.

Melody Maker

August 25, 1979   18p weekly   USA: one dollar

THE GLORY BOYS AND THE NEW NARCISSISM

The nouveau mods take the coast road

by CHRIS BOHN (p.17)

THE FORCE BOARDS IN TORQUAY/PIC: JILL FURMANOVSKI

MILLIONS LIKE US
Too late and much too early?

"Jam look/soundalikes The Chords celebrated the triumphant return from their sell-out world tour — it says here — with a Sixties soul party in SE London's hip Borough High Street. Anybody who is nobody was there." NME 31.3.79

That was how *New Musical Express* first acknowledged Britain's New Musical Happening and if you thought that was a tad negative, well hold on to your hats, there was worse to come. *NME* in particular seemed vehemently intent on heaping as much scorn as possible on to the scene and they did it while simultaneously plumbing previously uncharted depths of ignorance. But they weren't alone: practically every music paper in the country picked up the gauntlet, deriding and ridiculing anything that was even remotely associated with Mod. It was the first time I'd encountered such a backlash and I found it puzzling. After all, weren't these papers and their journos meant to encourage Britain's youth cultures, whatever their musical preferences? Worst of all it was all spat out in print right into the face of an overwhelming public opinion that quite obviously begged to differ, didn't it?

The Who's much-hyped film *Quadrophenia* was released on May 2, 1979, to the sort of box-office furore we now associate with big-budget blockbusters such as *Titanic*, *Star Wars* and *Toy Story*. The big difference was that films released in 1979 didn't come complete with an avalanche of merchandise. Although in *Quadrophenia's* case you could be forgiven for being mistaken, for within weeks of the film hitting the cinema, the entire nation seemed to be caught up once again in the grip of Modmania.

The first ones to cash in on the craze were the tacky tourist traps of Carnaby Street. They miraculously managed to transform their Great British Souvenir Fest into a Great British Mod Mountain, and anything with a Union Jack on it was instantly Mod, from tea mugs, tea towels and piggy banks in the shape of a pillar box to postcards, fridge magnets and beer glasses. You could buy big sew-on target patches with Who and Jam logos in the centre and even ready-customised parkas. The Carnaby Cavern went into complete overdrive and painted their shop front with a huge Union Jack, announcing they were the original Mod tailors to the stars, while the indoor market did away with all their afghan coats and post-punk bondage gear and replaced it with cheap button-down shirts and tonic jackets. Ads for Shelly's Jam shoes, Cavern Jam suits and Mod sew-ons filled the back pages of *NME*, warning the impulsive buyer to 'Beware of imitations — we are the best!'

Billy Hassett: *"When that film came out it was as if someone had done a fly-on-the-wall documentary in order to kill us all off. I went to see it at a cinema on Oxford Street and I came out depressed because I knew it was the end for us before we really got started. No London Mods had anything to do with it"*.

I was working at Decca Records at this time and would spend most lunch-times in a pub across the road from the office called The Dog and Trumpet which was on the corner of Carnaby Street and Great Marlborough Street. Here I would meet up with Gary Crowley, who now worked at *NME*, or Don Begley, who was working at a motorcycle shop on Great Portland Street. We'd get in a couple of pints before I had to report back and help arrange a press conference for Father Abraham, Wooly Rhino or one of the other cutting-edge signings that once-great label had managed to scoop. It was on one such lunch-time that I became fully aware of how far the whole Mod thing had come. Don came in with a huge smirk on his face gesturing wildly with his thumb over his shoulder and asking *"Have you seen outside?"*

"No."

"There's fucking hundreds of Mods."

Now I can only equate the next experience to the scene from *The Wizard Of Oz*, when Dorothy's house has just crash-landed in black and white and she opens the door to complete Technicolor. We rushed outside and sure enough, across the street, milling around the Shakespeare's Head Pub, were Mods — and there was a fucking lot of them. From there on in Mod was huge again, and just like before it was huge again for all the wrong reasons.

Fleet Street was quick to commence with its usual blitzkrieg exposés, fashion spreads and insights, just as it had following the 1964 seaside punch-ups. But whereas the original scene was given a bit of depth and background, the New Mod Movement would be treated as little more than a film-influenced fad.

AFTER THE FILM THE BANDS WILL COME

Gary Sparks: *"I knew that following the film suddenly there would be bands coming out everywhere and I was right... to be honest, most of them were crap."*

It would be oh-so convenient continuity-wise if I could rewrite history and this chapter heading could turn out to be true. But that, unfortunately, isn't the case. And it wouldn't really be fair anyway, because the truth is there were a number of Mod bands around BQ (Before *Quadrophenia*), such as the aforementioned Scooters and The Points. Back To Zero, Long Tall Shorty, The Teenbeats and The Killermeters were all bands that had a bit of history behind them by 1979. There were a couple who had undergone a name change and an image tweak, like The New Hearts, who became Secret Affair, and The Sneakers who turned into The Merton Parkas, but even these bands had put some time in. No, the problem was the blatancy with which some bands or individuals cashed in on the scene.

Billy Hassett: *"It wasn't so much that bands or people jumped on a Mod bandwagon, that's inevitable with any popular music outbreak. Even punk went a bit wishy-washy... second and third wave punk like The Lurkers, The Upstarts and things like the Anti-Nowhere League. It was more the way some of the little bands that were playing around very low-key suddenly lost all self-respect for themselves and went all out. I'm not saying you shouldn't seize an opportunity when it arises, but do it with a bit of integrity. A few bands had*

careers planned. We were recording an album, so were the Hearts. It was long term for us, we were in for the hard slog. It wasn't a gimmick like it was for some. It was like, 'Good God, where have all these people come from?' That film gave a lot of little bands the chance to be big for a very short time and some record companies turned it all into a race: fuck the content, be first. It was no different from punk. Record labels had got caught out first time, so they signed anything that swore. Look at The Stranglers. My God, they weren't punk. It goes back to the Sixties in that respect. Record labels turning down Mersey Beat: 'Fuck me did we? Quick, sign Mersey Beat.' The same thing happened again, that's why labels don't sign bands any more. It's easier to make your own."

When any youth-based cult gets as big as Mod did first and second time around, you'll eventually hear from the people who say that they started it all. They'll always carp on about how it was never meant to be a mass-marketed movement and that once it was, it was over. I've read the articles about the Bromley Contingent moaning about being the first punks and how it was all ruined once punk was commercialised. What was it Mark Perry (*Sniffin' Glue* editor) said? *"Punk died the day The Clash signed a record contract."* Steve Strange and his Blitz Club crowd were forever bemoaning the popularity of their New Romantic revolution. Even the Manchester baggy scene and the bands from The Haçienda — to hear some of them talk you'd believe that whole scene died as early as the morning of the Munich air disaster. It doesn't seem to happen now, mainly because music-based cults or youth movements have pretty much become a thing of the past.

So it's hard to explain why these people felt so impassioned about being originators, ace faces or scene leaders, other than to say that when you're young, it matters. I'm getting very close to cliché here, but no-one wants to be just a 'face in the crowd', and Mod was becoming a pretty big crowd.

Buddy Ascott: *"Identity is important, or was important to these people. They felt elite because to be elite is rare, and rarity is valuable. It's esoteric and all that's taken away if something becomes mainstream."*

Grant Fleming: *"I'm not saying I was the first Mod in the Seventies, but I was the first Mod down West Ham."*

The Jam were about the biggest band in Europe by the end of 1979 and Weller was (reluctantly and unintentionally) the voice of the people. Jam gigs were Mod meccas and the audience was a sea of green parkas, targets and arrows. I must admit, I felt a pang of resentment in being lumped in with all these newcomers. The press, on the back of the film, had made up their minds that Mods were a backward-looking bunch of plagiarist luddites and, there was no budging them. To be fair, some of the bands and the events they took part in during those first few months following *Quadrophenia*'s release didn't help matters.

The Sneakers (*not* The Sneakers in the film), now renamed The Merton Parkas, summed it up in a nutshell for *NME* and their ilk. The band's debut single, 'You Need Wheels', by a cruel twist of fate became the whole Mod scene's debut 45, and made them the first Mod band on *TOTP*. If that wasn't tantamount to giving *NME* a stick to beat us all with, I don't know what was. Many a time I cringed in embarrassment while walking down Oxford Street with taunts of *"Oi, you need wheels, mate"* ringing in my crimson ears.

Then there was the tour. 'The March of the Mods' tour was a cheap package affair that lumped as many Mod bands together as possible and in which The Purple Hearts unwisely participated, and the album *Mods Mayday*, which crammed in even more. These two examples put a firm lid on any chance of a maturing musical future for any of the participants. They might as well have been called the 'Shelf Life of Mod Tour' and the 'Sell By' album.

Buddy Ascott: *"I don't blame the Merton Parkas, I blame the people who bought it. I mean, come on — 'You Need Wheels', was that really our 'Anarchy In The UK'?"*

MARCH OF THE MODS
Purple Hearts   BACK TO ZERO   SECRET AFFAIR

TOUR DATES

August 10	Scarborough — Penthouse	August 24	W. Runton — Pavillion
August 14	Plymouth — Clones	August 26	London — Lyceum
August 15	Torquay — Townhall	*August 27	Canvey Paddocks
August 20	Swansea — Circles Club	August 28	Sheffield — Limit
August 16	Birmingham — Barbarellas	August 29	Barnsley — Civic
August 17	Manchester — Factory	August 30	Leeds — Fforde Grene
August 18	Cheltenham — Whitcombe Lodge	August 31	Newcastle — Mayfair
August 22	Newport — Stowaway	September 1	Liverpool — Eric's
August 23	Bristol — Trinity Leisure Centre		

This tour has been arranged by Cowbell

PUBLICITY SHOT CURIOUSLY STAGED OUTSIDE BRIAN POOLE'S BUTCHERS SHOP IN MANOR PARK.

THE CHORDS' FIRST PHOTO SESSION, GREENWICH, 1978.

The Merton Parkas shouldn't carry the can alone, for there were others equally guilty of turning Mod into the dirty three-letter word it became so quickly. The Lambrettas rocketed out of nowhere to lay claim to the second Mod 45 release with their cover of 'Poison Ivy'. This resulted in another *TOTP* appearance by a Mod band, which meant the words 'parka' and 'Lambretta' were now well and truly burnt into the public conscience. Subtlety was not at work here. I don't recall punk bands calling themselves The Safety Pins or The Pogos, do you? Then came the others: The Mods (discreet!); Squire, our very own Stranglers; The Fixations and The Distant Echo. God, the list seemed endless. Shouts of bandwagon jumpers were loud; groups that were still to release singles, such as The Chords and The Hearts, found themselves in the awkward position of having to publicly distance themselves from the scene and their fans while almost pathetically appealing to all fans of music to give them a chance, knowing full well the scene they had done so much to kick-start had run ahead of them.

And the person running the fastest was Ian Page, frontman of Secret Affair. Page was the self-proclaimed spokesman for the Mod generation and his rallying cry was their debut single *Time For Action*, a natty Mod anthem that told us all that *"looking good was the answer."*

Buddy Ascott: *"He called himself that, nobody else did. A bottle over the head became the answer, thanks to him."*

By the time The Chords and The Purple Hearts did eventually release singles they were pretty much assured of hits, but at what cost? The Chords appeared on *TOTP* three times and embarked on a nationwide tour as special guests of The Undertones. The Hearts didn't fare quite as well, due to their smaller label deal (they were still on the indie label Fiction, while The Chords had moved to Polydor) but they still managed to get TV and radio coverage. I didn't see a lot of either band during 1980, but I followed their respective careers intently via the continued bad press they and all the Mod groups generated. It was no longer being described as retro rubbish.

Simon Stebbing: *"We wanted to be seen as just another band not a so-and-so band. We knew we had to disassociate ourselves from it, the same as The Chords did, even though it was what we wanted to be. But we saw it as the death to come out with a record after Mod had blown up into this big thing. We saw the end from the beginning, but we didn't get out. Fucking hell, we were all about 17 at the time. What did we know, really?"*

Now it was just plain rubbish, full stop! Articles with headlines such as 'We're a Garbage Band' or 'For Sale, One Scooter, Barely New' were commonplace and did nothing to alter the country's perception of Mod. What made this all the more galling was the fact that outside of Mod the country was in the throws of huge rock-a-billy and ska revivals.

There were Stray Cats, Pole Cats, Hep Cats and Darts everywhere; Specials, Bodysnatchers and Madness too. And were these bands or their followings getting a hard time press-wise? Not on your life. Press and media darlings one and all, and never the merest mention of retro.

Simon Stebbing: *"We were doing gigs with Madness, The Specials and Selecter all supporting us and within a fortnight they were all number one or two. So that's quite amusing, you could dine out on that one!"*

I had my second encounter with Who boss Mr. Townshend and my first with ex-Small Face (and new

We saw the end fr

e beginning, but we didn't get out.

PHIL DANIELS AS 'JIMMY'
FROM THE FILM *QUADROPHENIA*

LONG TALL SHORTY, 1981
(L-R: TONY PERFECT, JOHN KIELY, DERWENT, STEWART ENGLAND).

Who drummer) Kenney Jones in March 1980. Gary Crowley was now working for a media company that did promotion for a lot of the big acts of the early Eighties, including The Pretenders and The Jam and, on this occasion, Pete Townshend. Townshend had a solo single out called 'Rough Boys', which featured Kenney Jones on drums. Both were appearing on the *Kenny Everett Video Show* and Townshend had asked for real Mods to be seen dancing in the audience. Gary knew just where to find some.

The deal was free beer and transport to and from the studio in White City, which seemed reasonable enough. What hadn't been explained however, was that Townshend had also requested a gang of Rockers to complete the picture.

A double-decker bus loaded with beer was laid on and as a small measure of segregation, the Rockers were put on the bottom and the Mods on the top. Sounds explosive? Well, not really. Rockers of the Eighties variety were a completely different animal to their Sixties leather-clad counterparts. These Rockers were of the heavy rock denim assortment, all stretch jeans and Iron Maiden T-shirts and, oh yes, cardboard guitars. They all had cardboard guitars for a bit of the ol' air-guitaring malarky. They were a very sad sight indeed. We even let them have the beer.

Eventually the relentless bad press afforded the new Mod bands throughout 1980, began to reflect in their record sales.

Billy Hassett: *"The Purple Hearts had a single called 'Millions Like Us'. Dozens like us more like, judging by the chart position."*

This caused the less hardy outfits, such as Back To Zero, The Mods and The Fixations, to zip up their parkas and call it a day by the end of the year. Paul Weller and The Jam kept ahead of any backlash by outwitting the reviewers and releasing one brilliant single after another, assuring their meteoric ascension into British rock history, and scoring several number ones along the way. This left their closest scene rivals, Secret Affair, trailing well behind in the chart stakes. The Chords and The Purple Hearts were struggling gamely on but even they were quietly conceding it was a one-horse race and looming defeat was awaiting them in the fame game. This was particularly true of The Chords, who'd just had their big break cruelly snatched away from them when their most important appearance on *TOTP* was cancelled due to a technicians' strike at White City.

Billy Hassett: *"The single 'Maybe Tomorrow' had gone in at number 40 after we did* Top Of The Pops *and all the signs were great. It was going Top 30 and another appearance would have pushed it into the Top Twenty and from there it should have been plain sailing. But the strike meant we couldn't go on and that was the same week that* Sounds *and the* NME *went on strike. The same week, so the single didn't get reviewed either and by the time it did (single of the week in* Sounds*) it was a case of too little too late."*

Ironically the one thing that would finally finish off all the remaining Mod bands (bad luck and bad press aside) would be the Mods themselves. By the beginning of 1981, London had a Mod club running every night of the week from Monday through until Sunday, heralding a huge shift away from live bands towards vinyl. East London had venues such as The Electric Ballroom, Barons, Ilford Palais and The Pidgeons. West London had Sneakers, located at the Bush Hotel, while the West End still had The Whisky A Go Go and the 100 Club as well as Le Beat Route and the Phoenix, which operated out of the basement of The Phoenix pub in Cavendish Square. All these clubs featured a playlist policy that was strictly a mixture of Northern Soul and Motown.

Simon Stebbing: *"All those clubs would say 'We don't play any white music', you had to listen to black music only. You'd never hear a Purple Hearts or a Chords record played. I couldn't listen to Motown for years after The Purple Hearts, I couldn't bear it and before all those clubs I loved it. But even at our gigs the DJs started to play the same stuff every night, you'd do 200 gigs a year and every night they'd play Needle in the fucking Haystack. There was no way we could make music like that, we were only competent to make white rock music."*

Bob Morris was a DJ at one of these clubs, the second coming of the Crawdaddy Club. This time the venue was situated in the less than salubrious Royal Oak, Whitechapel. *"The music was veering more and more towards Northern Soul, which in turn attracted a different sort of crowd,"* he recalled. *"The clubs went from being very smart to what many termed as 'Scruffy Northern' with people wearing army greens, deck steppers and T-shirts. Some clubs like The Electric Stadium even went through a phase of playing Edwin Starr's 1972 hit 'Eye to Eye Contact', which the Mods thought was an aberration, which it was. That's why we opened The Crawdaddy, to return to playing proper R&B and jazz. The entrance was strictly smart dress only and the word spread right across England to the West Country, even Scotland. The Mods started to get sussed again and other clubs started to restrict the entry to smart suits. Sneakers in Shepherds Bush had punch-ups outside every week, with people wearing trainers or army greens being refused entry."*

These clubs effectively divided the scene into three clearly defined factions. First off you had the new club-orientated Mods who called themselves purists. They all but abandoned the scooters and only entertained authentic Sixties R&B and Motown. Then you had the scooter scene, which was mainly the Northern Soul scene. This bore scant resemblance to Mod — it was all army combat trousers and Dr. Marten boots; even Mohican haircuts were starting to appear. This left a sort of everyday Mod sandwiched somewhere in-between. These were the gig-goers that were considered too casual for the trendy clubs and too Mod for the scooterists. The live music circuit in London, especially on a small club level, was now deemed an uncool waste of an evening by the purists and scooterists alike and this was at a time when the 100 Club in particular was putting on regular gigs by the inspirational likes of Jimmy McGriff, Billy Boy Arnold and Memphis Slim, the very people the purists were listening to on vinyl. I even saw one of Ronnie Lane's last English dates with his band Big Dipper at the 100 Club, a spectacle I shared

Modybodys' Meet, Mingle and Mingle In Modybody...... ways at the Modybody R&b Centre i.e.......

CRAWDADDY R&B CLUB ·········

Thursday, 28th March 1985. Admission £1.50 (sorry!)
At the cellar bar, THE Metropolitan, Farringdon Road
W.C.2.
D·J's Paul (I get everywhere) Hallam & guest's
Late night 9·p·m· till 1a·m· [Strictly smart dress, No jeans]

▶Friday At the top room, Royal Oak
Whitechaple High St. (⊖ Whitechaple), Adm £1.
D·J's Bob (I write sounds) Morris, Andy (tor the kids) orr
& Also someone called Eddie Pillor!
From 8·00 till 11·00 [Smart dress no happies]

Saturday The cellar at the Ben Trumen
Bar, ▶▶ Southwark Bridge Road
Southwark, (⊖ Bank)
D·J's Andy (init tor the kids) orr, Paul (I love money) H...
Plus Guests
Admission £1·50 [Smart dress, No jeans, No greens]!
. A Modybuy = A person or group of people that are
very smart, very lively, very hip & above all ve...
very very Mod!*··········

That's why we opened The Crawdaddy,

NINE BELOW ZERO (WITH DENNIS GREAVES AT FRONT).

with no more than 20 other paying punters. There were a few bright moments band-wise, like the formation of ex-Nine Below Zero's Dennis Greaves' soulful five piece The Truth. They scored a couple of Top 20 hits before unfair accusations of calculatingly attempting to fill the void left by the recently disbanded Jam, brought about their demise. The Rage, a Purple Hearts/Chords collaboration, were also a promising prospect, but the members deliberated for so long over which label to sign to that all interested parties eventually looked elsewhere. Both groups were brilliant while they lasted but it's safe to say that by 1984 the whole scene was a sad, dwindling affair, made all the more dismal by the brief period of violence that saw some ugly scenes (especially in south London) of fights between — now get this — Casuals and Mods!

What were Casuals? Well, Casuals were your average everyday working-class lad, whose normal world of designer labels, football and beer was the same world we all lived in, an ordinary one. They were simply members of Joe Public, albeit Joe Public with a cult name. Now this makes a difference, because once a cult gets a name, the next (il)logical step is to find an enemy and so — lo and behold — there came the dawning of the age of 'Mods and Casuals'. Doesn't roll off the tongue in quite the same way as 'Mods and Rockers', does it? And why might that be?

The answer's pretty obvious, and ironic to boot. These so-called Casuals were nothing more than an Eighties

version of Mod. They wore what was the height of good quality fashion, had neat, smart haircuts, were clean, hard and above all intent on looking better than the next guy up at the bar. Sound familiar? You bet it does. Casual was Mod's natural progression, only no-one saw it at the time, so the punch-ups carried on, until one day I heard some poor kid was finally killed when he was knocked off his scooter in the Old Kent Road.

By the mid-Eighties the whole Mod movement, in London at least, was as underground as it was possible to get without being buried. It was more like a little close-knit community that revolved around one or two club nights dotted around the capital and a handful of almost guerrilla-type Mod outfits that fought gamely on, regardless of any or no interest. Bands such as the irrepressible Long Tall Shorty, The Moment and The Scene valiantly kept the flame alive.

There was also the underground press. Well, a fanzine. *Extraordinary Sensations* was written by the self-proclaimed ace face of Essex, Eddie Piller who, to give credit where credit's due, almost single-handedly shook some life and enthusiasm back in to the lifeless corpse of the London Mod scene via the fanzine and his record label 'Well Suspect'.

Eddie came with good Mod credentials, too. His mum Fran had run The Small Faces Fan Club back in the Sixties and his aunt Pam had done the same for the short-lived High Numbers one. Eddie had also been one of the four little kids in the Small Faces 'Itchycoo Park' press ads of 1967. He was a good few years younger than the remaining Mods from the late Seventies revival, but he could still lay claim to having seen just about every band that had been and gone and he was now championing a handful of groups that were representative of what was already being termed 'the third wave of Mod'. This embraced bands that I'd never heard of until I met him, such as Les Elite, Directions, The Kick and Fast Eddie. He had already assembled a compilation album entitled

FRAN & YVONNE
"THE SMALL FACES FAN CLUB"
18 THE DELL
WOODFORD WELLS
ESSEX

turn to playing proper R&B and jazz.

5 4 3 2 1 GO

EDDIE PILLER.

The Beat Generation And The Angry Young Men, which collected together most of them, for which he asked me to design some sleeve artwork. Eddie's vision was to corral just about every remaining Mod group from both generations and create one huge like-minded roster, in much the same way Immediate Records had done back in the Sixties. He even suggested that he and I went out and looked for fresh talent. The label was to be Countdown Records and our first signing was a young band from the Midlands called 'Makin' Time'.

Countdown quickly gained the reputation as being Mod's final refuge (some say 'resting') place. A self-contained, Mod Mod world that signed any band that wore desert boots. And why not? We weren't spending our own money, we were spending Stiff Records' money. Stiff Records, the street-smart resurrection of pub rock, a label that had foisted the likes of Ian Dury, Elvis Costello and Nick Lowe on to the world stage in the midst of the punk rock revolution.

They had enjoyed several years of prosperous post-rock activity, most notably with Madness, their biggest earner of the Eighties. They liked the idea of having Countdown as a little subsidiary and of course we jumped at the chance. The only trouble was, that unbeknown to us, Stiff were completely skint.

We got the deal together with the help of the mighty Paul Conroy's ex-wife Maxine whom I had worked for at another label, called Sire Records.

Paul had been one of the main men behind Stiff in its heyday. This was before he moved on to seemingly govern the entire industry. Maxine was still friendly with Stiff's then head-honcho, Dave Robinson and she and Ed brokered the deal on the back of our little Midland Mods, Makin' Time.

Eddie Piller: *"They were the only Mod band at the time that I could relate to and I don't mean on a musical level. They had the whole bit, the purist attitude, the clothes, scooters, everything. Martin's brother was really into the scooter scene and I went on a lot of the runs with him."*

They had the whole bit, the purist attitude, the clothes, scooters, everything.

did. Don't get me wrong, I liked Makin' Time and their manager Will Birch who was the ex-drummer with another pub rock outfit, The Kursal Flyers, but to be honest they were an unlikely looking bunch. First there was the angelic 16-year-old vocalist and organist Fay Hallam, the only female on the entire circuit. (If you discount Fast Eddies' delightful backing singers). But she came as a package with boyfriend and bass player Martin, a gentle and deep-thinking lad from the black stuff who had already coined their sound as rhythm and soul, a term that excited Ed no end. Bizarre.

Then there was guitar player and lead vocalist Mark Govden who came from South-east Asia. So he was rechristened 'Sid' to give him a more down-to-earth quality. Lastly there was Neil Clitheroe, a little Freddy Garity character, who was the most unlikely drummer I'd yet laid eyes on.

Still, they were all we had and we wanted to make the most of them, so with Will Birch's pop knowledge (he had also been in power pop pretties The Records) and a handful of original numbers the band went into the studio and emerged with what was almost the first Mod

Eddie Piller: *"The single came out at the same time as Katrina and the Waves' had hit the big time with 'Walking on Sunshine'* and Makin' Time had that same *sort of upbeat summer feel to it. It got massive air play but the single wouldn't move, it was something like 103 for weeks on end."*

Despite the poor chart showing of Makin' Time's debut, Countdown had got off to a good start. We signed The Prisoners, a hammond organ-driven garage/Mod band from the outerworldly 'Snodland' and another band called The Kick.

We sent the whole lot out on the road in true Stiff package tour tradition and sat back and waited for the fab reviews to spark off yet another Mod Renewed Renewal. And nothing happened!

The music press, it seemed, had long grown bored of rubbishing anything to do with Mod. Instead they chose a new tack. Now they would simply ignore it altogether in the hope that starved of any critical column inches, the whole package would quite simply give up and

MARTIN BLUNT AT THE 100 CLUB
(DREAMING OF A BETTER FUTURE).

go home. The Smiths, New Order and Simple Minds were top of the mainstream menu and anything that harked back to the Sixties was considered more out of time than Makin' Time.

And with that in mind, once again it was left to the Mods themselves to make things worse. Some of the more obvious Mod club venues up and down the country refused to let the bands play, claiming they weren't in tune with their purist ethics, a move that drastically cut down any chances of this new scene breaking out of its minority status.

Despite this the bands gigged gamely on and all began to build a solid following in most of the big towns in the UK and Ireland, ably supported by each city's various little Mod societies and fanzines.

Eddie Piller: *"It was building up very nicely, all the bands played their own gigs everywhere and they were getting bigger and bigger and all with absolutely no press or promotion. The only time we did manage to get any press was when we literally packed a coach full of beer and invited journalists from everywhere up to Birmingham, all expenses paid, to watch Makin' Time, who were easily the biggest live band up there then. We took a lot of the London scene's faces up as well and the whole thing turned into a nightmare when all the local Brummie scooter boys turned up and tried to smash the pub to pieces. There was the biggest fight ever and all these journos were covered with flying glass and blood. Not one of them wrote a word."*

To say all these bands and the Mod movement itself in the Eighties were prisoners of their own fate, makes it all sound awfully poetic. However, it was obvious that it was out of step with just about everything, everywhere. Trapped in a musical history equivalent of the dark ages, far too late for Mod's first flurry of revivalist bands and far too early for the Nineties all-accepting and appreciative, successful and generally older Modsters.

Despite the huge up-hill struggle, Countdown and its happy (well not very happy – The Prisoners were now crediting me and Eddie for ruining their careers) roster of groups worked hard for the next six months hoping for a break or at least a shift in fashion. And it actually looked like it might happen, especially with Makin'

Time, who were now pulling in 500-plus punters a night on the Continent. That's when we found out Stiff had no money.

Countdown and many of the groups folded up under heavy debts. We sent out end of an era party invites that showed a cheery picture of a real life suicide and that was just about that. Eddie relocated and re-invented the label with what was originally a spoof title, Acid Jazz.

Acid Jazz quickly became more than just a record label. It transformed into its very own scene machine, comprising DJs, clubs, magazines and happenings. It successfully fused together a whole plethora of musical styles from straight jazz and Latin dance to cheesy TV and film themes and even good ol' R&B. This diverse musical pot-pourri gave rise to a strange, hybrid Mod style that drew obvious inspiration from the jazz scene but combined it with equal parts Beatnik, Casual and Mod. The labels initial signings, such as the James Taylor Quartet and Mother Earth, were mostly the remnants of ex-Countdown outfits like The Prisoners (Jamie Taylor, Alan Crockford) or The Kick (Chris White) plus a handful

A PRIME EXAMPLE OF THE ACID JAZZ / MOD CROSSOVER.

of Mod revivalists and acquaintances. Eventually the roster expanded and began to attract younger musicians and groups that were not instantly associated with Mod or its ephemera, such as the Brand New Heavies and Jamiroquai, whose high-profile careers catapulted the label into the big leagues. These types of acts, and the Acid Jazz scene itself, mirrored perfectly just how thoroughly Mod had seeped into the country's sub-conscious. Even the Northern scooter scene no longer seemed the grebo mishmash of army greens and Dr. Martens that had become its trade mark; instead it had become the source of an integrated network of talent and personalities that were forging a new and vibrant scene all of their own.

Groups were being formed all over the north of England, on the back of the scooter clubs, by the likes of Ian Brown and John Squire – two confirmed scooter enthusiasts – while idealist record company boss Alan McGee was setting up his label, Creation. This was aptly named after his favourite Sixties pop art pioneers who, in a bizarre twist of fate, would eventually reform and sign up with him. They in turn would take their place alongside other distinctly Mod-tinged groups, such as McGee's own outfit Biff Bang Pow and Ed Ball and his one-time Countdown contributors The Times. There was even a success story happening a little closer to home with ex-Makin' Time bass player Martin Blunt's new band, The Charlatans. They were about to make the transition from indie hopefuls to bona-fide rock stars, helped on their way I might add (and I'm sure Martin would be the first to admit this) by a couple of pointers regarding the Hammond-led sound gleaned from his old label mates The Prisoners and personal favourites The Truth. It would take a little while for all these young bloods to take up their rightful places in the great scheme of British Rock, and when they did they found they were not alone. They had been joined by other unashamed Mod influenced contenders, all of whom had been steadily bringing up the rear, bands such as Blur, Oasis and Ocean Colour Scene, who it seemed, couldn't get through an *NME* article without namechecking The Small Faces, The Kinks and the by now undisputed Modfather for our generation, Paul Weller.

So how come all these latter-day household names are allowed to wear their Mod hearts and colours on their sleeves so openly and with such respectful pride, without a spiteful journalistic savaging? The answer is time, my friends – time, it seems, has finely rounded the edges of retrospection. All of these bands, with the obvious exception of Paul Weller, currently exist in a pop/rock music climate that is further away from the advent of punk rock in terms of years than the 1979 clutch of bands were away from the break-up of The Beatles. Back in the late Seventies The Beatles (and most of their contemporaries for that matter) were not considered the revered heroes they are now... just ask Glen Matlock. No sir, in the days of punk, and its heady aftermath, bands of The Beatles' ilk were the enemy – hated, bearded hippies. In fact, if you admitted liking any band from the Sixties you risked having your head put on a spike, so a whole movement that derived from a deep love of that most magical era naturally became detested. Nowadays Mod is an everyday term, as solidly a part of our society as Coleman's mustard, bangers and mash and cricket on the green. Its elements are woven into the nation's very fabric and its imagery is everywhere you look – scooters and scooter-riding Mods are used to advertise and push everything from Lucozade to tampons. Mods are always the stock, fail-safe fashion spread in just about every lifestyle magazine available, and the humble target design is a staple of a thousand logos and corporate IDs from popular TV shows such as *Shooting Stars* to commercial operations like Parcel Force.

So there you pretty much have it. I hope you weren't expecting too much of a heavy sociological insight into this very British phenomenon. It wasn't possible to include everything and everyone, despite such obvious influences as Northern Soul, etc – there simply wasn't the space. Suffice to say, Mod has certainly endured its lean years, but it has eventually emerged triumphant – the only British teenage youth cult to have done so.

Gary 'Mani' Mounfield (Stone Roses and Primal Scream):
"We were made for Tamla and Northern Soul and we didn't give a shit what anyone else thought, and if anyone did slag us off we would have fucking chinned them. I've still got my scooter, a Lambretta SX200 white standard, it's a fucking knicker-dropping machine. Mod influenced us all, even now for sure – Temps, Four Tops, The fucking Who, awesome! Entwistle, brilliant apart from the beard!"

Bobby Gillespie (Jesus & Mary Chain and Primal Scream):
"We were all big Who fans. One of the first albums I bought was 'Meaty, Beaty, Big and Bouncy'. I never knew what Mods were back then, around '76, so I became a punk. A year or two later there was Mods and punks and I think they both had the same sort of aesthetic – sharp, violent, angry, short haircuts, smart gear... everything's sharp, no round edges, everything's spiky. That's how it influenced us, that and the R&B side of thing, through Weller and The Jam covering 'Heatwave' and R&B stuff. My mum and dad's Motown and Stax record collection was another big influence. We covered Eddie Floyd's 'Big Bird'. I was always into pop art too. We've got a song called 'Swastika Eyes' which is a very pop art title, so all these influences are still with us."

Made in Britain

THANKS...
Kenney Jones and his mum, Richard Barnes, Graham Hughes, Paul Stagg, John 'Dicky' Dodso[...]
Ken Browne, Johnny Moke, Tony Lordan, Gary Crowley, Bob Morris, Buddy Ascot, Billy Hasse[...]
Martin Mason, Gary Sparks, Simon Stebbing, Dennis Greaves, Steve McNerny, Paul McEvoy,
Julie Anderson, Julien Potter, Kerry Oldham, Dan the scan Lidell, Mark Woolwich, Grant Fle[...]
Gered Mankowitz, Jean Louis Rancurel, Roch Vidal, Art Wood, Jan Olofsson, Dave Powell,
Mani Mounfield, Bobby Gillespie, Maxine Forrest, Eddie Piller, Paul Hallam, Gary Warren,
Lynn Simms, Little Diane, Ali McKenzie, Paul Yarett/Williams, Peter Stringfellow, Pat Jay,
Paul Newman, Guy Joseph, Keith Badman, Paddy Wilson, Beverly Dunn, Chris Charlesworth,
Steve Diggle, Adam Bishop, Andy Neil, Steve Carter, Dean Powell, Dean Rudland, Nigel Hoo[...]
Ady Crosdell, John @ Simons, Glynn Cunningham, Gary 'Lager' Copeland, Tony 'Boy Racer' P[...]
Troy Shanks, The East London & Essex Mods and all other Mods, past and present, even thos[...]
we've not necessarily loved...

Guy Joseph & Bob Morris for extra scooter info, and Bob again for extra research

Scooter pix thanks: Alan Balsham, PW Feldhahn, Anthony Redding, Linda La Roche, R Wood[...]
D Hughes, J Trewin, Kevin McDonald, KD Turner, John Ludlow, Joe Carpenter, Mark Sargean[...]
Bruce Gryckiewicz, Dave Dry, D Hemstock, John Hemstock, Mick Turner, KY Cairns, Paul CJ Fi[...]
J Reeves, Lee Durrant, Paul McBurnie, Steve Miller, Mark Baxter, Ken Browne, Dec Hallahan,
Dan Hughes, Bill Norwood, Dave Middleton.

Apologies to anyone I've inadvertantly missed out, of which I'm sure there are many.

Every effort has been made to trace and credit photographers and contributors where possi[...]

Design & artwork by Paul McEvoy & Julien Potter with Terry Rawlings
@ **BOLD** Graphic Design, London.

Special thanks to Lesley, Molly & Nancy Rawlings.

PICTURE CREDITS
Front cover: Graham Hughes.
Back cover picture of author: Justina Dewhurst Richins.

Inner pictures: Not Fade Away; Hulton Getty; Art Wood;
Peter Stringfellow; Ali McKenzie; Rex Features;
British Library; Roch Vidal; Jean Louis Rancurel;
Jan Olofsson; Kenney Jones; Tony Lordan;
Bob Morris; Simon Stebbing; Gary Sparks;
Buddy Ascot; Martin Mason; Billy Hassett;
Lynn Simms; Steve 'Chad' Fredericks; Paul Hallam;
Diane Port; Maxine Orr; Karen Malcolm;
Grant Fleming; Mark Woolwich.

424 BYT